Classics

SURREY

COUNTY CRICKET CLUB

Classics

SURREY

COUNTY CRICKET CLUB

JERRY LODGE

TEMPUS

First published 2006

Tempus Publishing Limited
The Mill, Brimscombe Port,
Stroud, Gloucestershire, GL5 2QG
www.tempus-publishing.com

British Library Cataloguing in Publication Data.
A catalogue record for this book is available from the British Library.

ISBN 0 7524 3786 0

Typesetting and origination by Tempus Publishing Limited.
Printed in Great Britain.

Acknowledgements

The majority of the photographs have been supplied from the Surrey County Club Photo Library in conjunction with Empics. If any photographic source believes it holds the copyright of any photograph reproduced in this book, it should contact the publisher, in the first instance, to rectify the matter.

Bibliography

Cowley, Brian (Ed), *Surrey County Cricket Club – First-Class and Limited Overs Records 1846-2000*, Surrey CCC, 2000.

Grace, W.G., *Cricket*.

Jones, Trevor, *268 – The Blow-by-Blow Account of Ali's Amazing Onslaught and the Day Records Tumbled*, Sporting Declaration Books, 2002.

Jones, Trevor, *The Dream Fulfilled*, Sporting Declaration Books, 2000.

Jones, Trevor, *Doubling Up with Delight*, Sporting Declaration Books, 2001.

Jones, Trevor, *From Tragedy to Triumph*, Sporting Declaration Books, 2002.

Lemmon, David, *The History of Surrey County Cricket Club*, Christopher Helm, 1989.

Lodge, Jerry, *100 Greats – Surrey County Cricket Club*, Tempus Publishing, 2003.

Lodge, Jerry, *Into the Second Century*, Tempus Publishing, 2004.

Murphy, Patrick, *Fifty Incredible Cricket Matches*, Stanley Paul, 1987.

Webber, J.R., *The Chronicle of W.G.*, The Association of Cricket Statisticians and Historians, 1998.

Preface

By the end of the 2005 season Surrey had played 3,429 first-class matches, so to pick out fifty of the finest has been an interesting challenge. Naturally, several of the best matches involve those years in which Surrey have won the County Championship, namely 1887 to 1892, 1894, 1895, 1899, 1914, 1952 to 1958, 1971, 1999, 2000 and 2002.

The most impressive run of success was from 1952 to 1958, under the inspired leadership of Stuart Surridge for the first five of those years followed by two years when Peter May was captain. This era has been duly reflected in that fourteen matches from this period have been included.

Surrey have been involved in many titanic struggles against their major opponents such as Kent, Middlesex, Nottinghamshire, Lancashire and Yorkshire over the years. The number of matches played against each county in the Championship has been:

Derbyshire	132	Leicestershire	150
Durham	10	Middlesex	254
Essex	179	Northamptonshire	110
Glamorgan	101	Nottinghamshire	238
Gloucestershire	205	Somerset	161
Hampshire	174	Sussex	261
Kent	267	Warwickshire	156
Lancashire	207	Worcestershire	117
Yorkshire	241		

Surrey have also had considerable success against Australian teams when they have visited England in Test match years. They have played against them 48 times and won on 9 occasions. Highlighted are matches played in 1886 and 1956, the latter match being the famous occasion when Jim Laker took 10 wickets in an innings. I was very happy to have been at the 1956 match and my most vivid memory is how hard Tony Lock was striving to take a wicket at the other end.

In recent years the County have played many one-day matches and these are represented by just one match, the incredible Cheltenham & Gloucester match against Glamorgan played at The AMP Oval in 2002 when many records were broken.

Some matches have been included that reflect historical personal performances, such as Jack Hobbs breaking the record of W.G. Grace in scoring the most centuries in first-class cricket against Somerset at Taunton in 1925 and Pat Pocock taking 7 wickets in 11 balls against Sussex at Eastbourne in 1972.

Naturally, it is inevitable that many people will disagree with my selection but, hopefully, those matches highlighted will reflect many aspects of the history of Surrey County Cricket Club.

Note: * denotes captain, # denotes wicketkeeper.

Classic Matches

1872   *v.* Gloucestershire at The Oval

1879   *v.* Sussex at The Oval

1886   *v.* The Australians at The Oval

1887   *v.* Nottinghamshire at The Oval

1888   *v.* Lancashire at Old Trafford

1888   *v.* Yorkshire at Bradford

1889   *v.* Yorkshire at The Oval

1894   *v.* Lancashire at The Oval

1906   *v.* Leicestershire at Leicester

1911   *v.* Northamptonshire at Northampton

1914   *v.* Yorkshire at Lord's

1919   *v.* Kent at The Oval

1920   *v.* Middlesex at Lord's

1925   *v.* Somerset at Taunton

1928   *v.* Nottinghamshire at Trent Bridge

1928   *v.* Kent at The Oval

1932   *v.* Middlesex at The Oval

1934   *v.* Middlesex at The Oval

1947   *v.* Nottinghamshire at Trent Bridge

1948   *v.* Lancashire at The Oval

1952   *v.* Kent at The Oval

1952   *v.* Middlesex at The Oval

1953   *v.* Warwickshire at The Oval

1953   *v.* Lancashire at Old Trafford

1953	v. Nottinghamshire at The Oval
1954	v. Northamptonshire at Kettering
1954	v. Worcestershire at The Oval
1955	v. Yorkshire at The Oval
1956	v. The Australians at The Oval
1956	v. Kent at Blackheath
1956	v. Yorkshire at Bramall Lane, Sheffield
1957	v. Northamptonshire at Northampton
1958	v. Worcestershire at Worcester
1959	v. Essex at The Oval
1971	v. Derbyshire at The Oval
1972	v. Sussex at Eastbourne
1987	v. Middlesex at The Oval
1994	v. Derbyshire at The Fosters Oval
1994	v. Gloucestershire at Gloucester
1995	v. Gloucestershire at The Fosters Oval
1995	v. Yorkshire at The Fosters Oval
1999	v. Hampshire at Guildford
2000	v. Hampshire at The Fosters Oval
2000	v. Leicestershire at Oakham School
2000	v. Leicestershire at Guildford
2001	v. Leicestershire at Leicester
2002	v. Glamorgan at The AMP Oval
2002	v. Kent at Canterbury
2004	v. Kent at The Brit Oval
2005	v. Glamorgan at The Brit Oval

Surrey v. Gloucestershire

Date: 3-4 June 1872

County Championship

Location: The Oval

W.G. Grace was at the highest point in his batting career when Gloucestershire arrived at The Oval under his captaincy having won their last four matches against Surrey. In his first-class career of 870 matches Grace played no less than 121 of them at The Oval, where he averaged 42.62 with the bat, scoring twenty centuries, and took 416 wickets at 17.49.

Winning the toss Grace went out with T.G. Matthews at noon to face the bowling of Marten and Southerton. However, it began to rain heavily and play did not start until 12.38 p.m. Grace was then clean bowled by a slow ball from Southerton that broke a long way from leg and took his off stump. Wickets fell quickly and when lunch was taken the score was 114 for 6. Rain delayed the restart until 3.25 p.m., and even then the light was bad and light rain was falling. When the score had reached 138 for 7 at 4 p.m. heavy rain stopped play for nearly an hour. Gloucestershire were eventually all out at 5.05 p.m. after an innings that lasted about two-and-a-half hours.

Surrey began their innings at 5.30 p.m. with Jupp and Humphrey scoring 60 runs in the first forty-five minutes. However, the next forty-five minutes told a completely different story as 5 wickets fell for only 13 runs. By the time stumps were drawn at 7 p.m. the score was 75 for 5, Brice having conceded only two singles from his last 13 overs.

The next day was glorious and play began at 12.15 p.m. However, few runs were accumulated by the lower order and the Surrey innings closed on 115, a deficit of 38. Grace and Filgate opened the Gloucestershire second innings and Grace hit the first ball to Freeman at deep mid-off but the youngster failed to hold it. The opening stand of 43 was terminated when Caffyn bowled Filgate. Six runs later Grace was bowled again by Southerton with a ball well pitched up that took his middle stump. At lunch the score was 58 for 3, but after play resumed at 3.15 p.m. the side collapsed, the last 7 wickets falling for 13 in fifty-five minutes. After the first-wicket partnership, 10 wickets had fallen for 28 runs and Gloucestershire were all out at 4.10 p.m. after rather less than two hours' batting. The ball kicked a good deal and after lunch Marten took 3 for 0 in 10 overs.

Surrey changed their batting order for the second innings with 110 needed to win. Freeman was bowled second ball and Hall followed soon after, a well-judged catch at square leg disposing of him in Grace's third

James Southerton.

over. Chester was then caught, leaving the score at 14 for 3. Humphrey and Jupp then put together a partnership of 60 until Jupp was dismissed. Two more wickets fell quickly but Caffyn and Humphrey advanced the total to 96 when both Caffyn and Palmer lost their wickets. Fourteen to win, two wickets left. Marten hit W.G. Grace for two and one in his next over, but only a single came in the next 6 overs. Marten hit Brice for four and then another 3 maidens followed. Humphrey was bowled at 108 and Southerton joined Marten. It was now 6.55 p.m., five minutes to stumps, and the excitement was intense. In the next over W.G. Grace bowled the first ball high to Marten. He tried to hit it but skied it to Miles at forward short leg, a very easy chance. He dropped it and the winning run, a leg bye, was made 4 balls later with two minutes to spare. The undoubted star of the match was James Southerton, taking 10 wickets in all, assisted by one catch and two stumpings from Edward Pooley.

SURREY *v.* GLOUCESTERSHIRE

Played at The Oval on 3rd and 4th June 1872 [3-day Match]   Toss: Gloucestershire
Surrey won by 1 wicket

GLOUCESTERSHIRE

*W.G. Grace	b Southerton	13	b Southerton		25
T.G. Matthews	st Pooley b Southerton	5	[6] c Marten b Southerton		0
C.S. Gordon	b Marten	2	c T. Humphrey b Caffyn		10
G.F. Grace	c Freeman b Caffyn	40	c T. Humphrey b Marten		7
G. Strachan	b Marten	35	c & b Marten		4
#J.A. Bush	b Southerton	13	[8] c Pooley b Southerton		0
C.R. Filgate	c Southerton b Marten	4	[2] b Caffyn		16
E.A. Brice	b Marten	13	[7] c Caffyn b Southerton		0
R.F. Miles	b Southerton	10	b Marten		1
E.K. Browne	st Pooley b Southerton	7	not out		3
H.S. Cobden	not out	5	c Jupp b Southerton		2
Extras	b 4, lb 1, w 1	6	b 1, lb 2		3
Total	**(all out)**	**153**	**(all out)**		**71**

SURREY

H. Jupp	c Bush b Brice	18	[4] c & b Brice		19
R. Humphrey	c Bush b Brice	42	[5] c Filgate b Strachan		42
W.T. Palmer	c & b W.G. Grace	0	[9] b Brice		0
T. Humphrey	b W.G. Grace	2	[8] b Brice		8
#E.W. Pooley	c Matthews b Brice	8	[6] st Bush b Strachan		3
A. Freeman	b Brice	1	[1] b Brice		0
W. Caffyn	st Bush b W.G. Grace	5	b Brice		8
A. Chester	c Matthews b W.G. Grace	4	[2] c Filgate b Brice		10
C.J. Hall	not out	9	[3] c Browne b W.G. Grace		3
W.G. Marten	b Brice	6	not out		9
J. Southerton	c Matthews b Brice	9	not out		0
Extras	b 3, lb 3, w 5	11	b 4, lb 1, nb 1, w 2		8
Total	**(all out)**	**115**	**(for 9 wickets)**		**110**

Bowling [4 balls per over]

SURREY	O	M	R	W	O	M	R	W
Marten	35	12	55	4	17	12	21	3
Southerton	42.2	13	71	5	28.3	15	32	5
Caffyn	7	0	21	1	11	4	15	2

GLOUCESTERSHIRE	O	M	R	W	O	M	R	W
Miles	6	2	15	0				
G.F. Grace	8	1	17	0	10	4	13	0
W.G. Grace	33	14	37	4	23	9	38	1
Brice	30.2	18	35	6	36.1	19	34	6
Strachan					13	7	17	2

FALL OF WICKETS

	G	S	G	S
1st	11	66	43	0
2nd	16	67	49	5
3rd	26	69	53	14
4th	86	69	63	74
5th	106	73	64	78
6th	112	86	64	79
7th	121	90	65	96
8th	140	90	66	96
9th	146	103	68	108
10th	153	115	71	—

Umpires: G. Griffith and C.K. Pullin

SURREY v. SUSSEX

Date: 4-6 August 1879   **County Championship**

Location: The Oval

James Southerton first played for Surrey in 1854 at the age of twenty-six. He played 70 matches for Sussex between 1858 and 1872 and 13 matches for Hampshire between 1861 and 1867. He played for all three counties in one season, qualifying by birth for Sussex and by residence for the other two. In June 1873 the county qualification rules were introduced and Southerton settled for Surrey as he was then the landlord of The Cricketers at Mitcham. Many of his finest performances took place late in his career and in Australia in 1876/77 he became the oldest player to make his Test debut at the age of forty-nine years and 119 days old, a record that stands to the present day and is most unlikely to be broken.

In his last season for Surrey he played in the match against Sussex at The Oval when he was fifty-one years 263 days old and had the magnificent match figures of 11 for 91 and, as so often, was ably supported by Pooley behind the stumps who caught two and stumped three of these eleven dismissals. It is generally agreed that no other wicketkeeper could have assisted Southerton to the extent that Pooley did. He was quick as lightning and, with all his brilliance, very safe. Partly from lack of opportunity he was not quite so good with very fast bowling, but to slow bowling he was, in his day, supreme.

According to the *Daily Telegraph*, Sussex won the toss and asked Surrey to bat; a big mistake by the Sussex captain H. Phillips. Two new players were introduced by Surrey in W.G. Wyld, who came from Dulwich College, and F.W. Bush, who had been playing well for Surrey Club and Ground. The first morning saw Surrey 78 for 1 at lunch, but the main contribution was a half-century by Walter Read although the seventh wicket fell at 194. Southerton, batting at number ten, scored 22 and with Emmanuel Blamires helped to add 28 runs for the last wicket.

Apart from an innings of 41 by the Sussex wicketkeeper Henry Phillips, only one other batsman reached double figures as Southerton and Joseph Potter shared all the wickets, Southerton bowling throughout the innings. The weather deteriorated on the second day with rain falling heavily just after 6 p.m.

Following on, Sussex lost their first 2 wickets for 6 runs, both to Southerton, Phillips being bowled for a duck. Sussex offered more resistance this time with some very good cricket, particularly involving H. Whitfield, down from Cambridge University. But in 67 four-ball overs James Southerton picked up 6

more wickets and bowled 43 maiden overs to see Surrey complete a comprehensive innings victory, the match finishing at 4.20 p.m.

At the end of the season Southerton was appointed superintendent of the ground bowlers, but his term of office was tragically brief as he died in June 1880 before reaching his fifty-second birthday. In his book *Cricket*, W.G. Grace described Southerton thus: 'His bowling was slow round-arm with a rather peculiar delivery, and by many players it was considered doubtful. On a rather sticky wicket he could get a great deal of work on the ball, and he was very clever in altering his pace and pitch. A trick of his was to deliver three balls, causing them to break six inches or more and then put in a fast straight one – a trick that was often successful. He had to be watched very closely: for he had a good head on his shoulders, and was continually seeking for a weak spot; and more than once I have seen him deliver the ball before he reached the crease.'

Walter Read.

SURREY v. SUSSEX

Played at The Oval on 4th, 5th and 6th August 1879 [3-day Match]   Toss: Sussex
Surrey won by an innings and 35 runs

SURREY

H. Jupp	c Howard b Lillywhite	34
*J. Shuter	b Pedley	3
L.A. Shuter	b Sharp	36
W.W. Read	c Greenfield b Lillywhite	53
J. Potter	c Greenfield b Sharp	5
R. Humphrey	c H. Phillips b Lillywhite	21
W.G. Wyld	lbw b Greenfield	28
F.W. Bush	run out	14
#E.W. Pooley	b Greenfield	9
J. Southerton	b Lillywhite	22
E. Blamires	not out	24
Extras	b 7, lb 5, w 2	14
Total	**(all out)**	**263**

SUSSEX

F.F.J. Greenfield	c Blamires b Southerton	9	b Southerton		4
W.E. Pedley	st Pooley b Southerton	10	(4) c Pooley b Southerton		15
#H. Phillips	c Potter b Southerton	41	b Southerton		0
H. Whitfield	c Potter b Southerton	1	(2) c Pooley b Southerton		31
J. Phillips	b Southerton	1	c Pooley b Blamires		5
C. Howard	c Pooley b Potter	6	b Read		36
*C. Sharp	lbw b Potter	1	st Pooley b Southerton		12
H.R.J. Charlwood	b Potter	3	st Pooley b Southerton		9
W.H. Millard	c Read b Potter	0	b Read		26
A. Smith	b Potter	0	not out		0
J. Lillywhite	not out	3	b Potter		1
Extras	b 3, lb 1, nb 1	5	b 5, lb 3, nb 1		9
Total	**(all out)**	**80**	**(all out)**		**148**

Bowling [4 balls per over]

SUSSEX	O	M	R	W
Lillywhite	65	42	47	4
Sharp	53	32	48	2
Greenfield	39.3	19	50	2
Pedley	38	14	69	1
Smith	31	16	35	0

SURREY	O	M	R	W	O	M	R	W
Southerton	44	19	38	5	67	43	53	6
Potter	26	17	14	5	43.2	25	40	1
Blamires	18	11	23	0	39	24	42	1
Read					3	0	4	2

FALL OF WICKETS

	Sur	Sus	Sus
1st	11	10	6
2nd	80	36	6
3rd	84	54	49
4th	95	56	59
5th	142	73	70
6th	161	74	85
7th	194	74	101
8th	209	74	141
9th	235	80	148
10th	263	80	148

Umpires: W. Caffyn and C. Payne

SURREY v. THE AUSTRALIANS

Date: 20-22 May 1886
Location: The Oval

This was the first time that Surrey had beaten the Australians and was an occasion marked by a visit from the Prince of Wales who, as the Duke of Cornwall, was the landlord of the Club, the land being part of the Duchy of Cornwall.

There was rain on the first day and Surrey batted while the wicket was easy. The innings lasted for three hours twenty minutes with eight of the batsmen reaching double figures. Maurice Read played capital cricket and Lohmann was in excellent form, scoring 46 out of 61 while at the wicket. Play had started at 12.15 p.m. after Australia had lost the toss, with Spofforth being unable to play due to illness. Play stopped for rain at 12.50 p.m., causing a break until 3 p.m.

Having been 12 for 2 overnight the last 8 Australian wickets fell on the second morning. Before a crowd of about 12,000 (10,305 paid), Lohmann bowled well as Australia were dismissed for 82, 9 of the wickets being bowled, the tenth being lbw. Lohmann finished with 6 wickets for 36. The score was 77 for 9 at lunch but only 5 runs were added on the resumption before Blackham was bowled by Lohmann.

Following on, Giffen batted for two hours forty minutes for his 54 not out and gave only one difficult chance in an admirable display of sound and judicious batting. Three wickets fell for 37 before fine resistance came from Giffen, Bonnor and Blackham. Blackham scored freely but at 31 Jones was bowled by his namesake and Scott's stay was brief, being stumped when score was 34. Jarvis played on at 37 so 3 wickets were down still 52 runs short of making Surrey bat again. Giffen and Blackman brought up the fifty. In the bowling, Beaumont replaced Lohmann and at 67 Blackham was caught at mid-on. A double change of bowling introduced Bowley and Abel which brought success as Bonnor was clean bowled by Bowley with the score at 114. Beaumont took over from Abel and bowled Palmer in his third over. Giffen gave a difficult chance to Beaumont at mid-on when 40, but then Jones bowled Bruce. Garrett was missed at slip and at the close of play the score was 172 for 9.

There was a heavy thunderstorm on the last morning and the wicket, though never very difficult, suffered appreciably from the downpour. Surrey had been set 83 to win and the Australians bowled and fielded very well. Surrey lost their first 3 wickets for 19 and the score rose steadily with Lohmann coming in with 16 runs still required. He was able to steer Surrey home with time to spare.

The bowling and fielding of the Australians was very fine. Only 10 runs were accumulated in fifteen minutes and then Shuter was caught at silly mid-off. Diver was caught at slip and then Walter Read, trying to attack, was caught at extra mid-off to the great dismay of the crowd; 19 for 3. Maurice Read came in and made only one stroke in the first 4 overs. After one hour the score had only risen to 30 and lunch was taken at 38 for 4 as Maurice Read was bowled.

After lunch Roller came in with Abel. As the fifty came up at 2.55 p.m. Abel was caught and Lohmann came to the wicket to support Roller. He played some exciting cricket to add 18 runs with him and then a further 10 with Wood. Jones and Lohmann then saw Surrey home. It had been a stoutly fought match that Australia looked like winning but the vigorous hitting by Roller, Lohmann and Wood won the match for Surrey amid great excitement.

John Shuter.

SURREY v. THE AUSTRALIANS

Played at The Oval on 20th, 21st and 22nd May 1886 [3-day Match]   Toss: Surrey
Surrey won by 3 wickets

SURREY

R. Abel	run out	24	c Jones b Garrett	13
*J. Shuter	c Jones b Evans	5	c Giffen b Evans	11
E.J. Diver	c Bonnor b Giffen	13	c Jones b Garrett	2
W.W. Read	b Palmer	14	c Bruce b Garrett	0
J.M. Read	b Evans	27	b Evans	14
W.E. Roller	b Garrett	14	b Evans	19
#H. Wood	run out	14	lbw b Giffen	8
G.A. Lohmann	not out	43	not out	8
G.G. Jones	c Blackham b Bruce	12	not out	4
T. Bowley	c Giffen b Garrett	2		
J. Beaumont	c Palmer b Evans	0		
Extras	b 1, lb 1, nb 1	3	b 5, lb 3	8
Total	**(all out)**	**171**	**(for 7 wickets)**	**87**

THE AUSTRALIANS

J.W. Trumble	b Lohmann	13	(2) c Wood b Beaumont	1
G.E. Palmer	lbw b Lohmann	2	(8) b Beaumont	1
E. Evans	b Lohmann	0	(11) c Wood b Jones	6
G.J. Bonnor	b Bowley	5	(6) b Bowley	34
S.P. Jones	b Bowley	14	(1) b Jones	6
*H.J.H. Scott	b Lohmann	5	(3) st Wood b Lohmann	0
G. Giffen	b Lohmann	4	(5) not out	54
T.W. Garrett	b Bowley	0	(10) c Roller b Jones	3
A.H. Jarvis	b Beaumont	19	(4) b Jones	1
#J.M. Blackham	b Lohmann	7	(7) c Jones b Beaumont	43
W. Bruce	not out	4	(9) b Jones	7
Extras	b 8, lb 1	9	b 12, lb 4	16
Total	**(all out)**	**82**	**(all out)**	**172**

Bowling [4 balls per over]

THE AUSTRALIANS	O	M	R	W	O	M	R	W
Evans	40.1	18	53	1	41.2	23	31	3
Giffen	22	6	41	1	3	1	3	1
Garrett	28	12	32	2	33	15	39	3
Palmer	22	9	29	1	5	2	6	0
Trumble	4	2	3	0				
Bruce	5	2	10	1				

SURREY	O	M	R	W	O	M	R	W
Lohmann	36	17	36	6	27	13	41	1
Beaumont	14	9	13	1	30	17	39	3
Bowley	24	14	24	3	22	11	26	1
Jones	3	3	0	0	27.2	14	34	5
Abel					3	0	16	0

FALL OF WICKETS

	S	A	A	S
1st	17	12	31	15
2nd	35	12	34	17
3rd	51	23	37	19
4th	71	33	67	38
5th	89	45	114	50
6th	110	47	117	68
7th	119	47	123	78
8th	146	71	146	–
9th	169	71	152	–
10th	171	82	172	–

Umpires: F.H. Farrands and C.K. Pullin

SURREY v. NOTTINGHAMSHIRE

Date: 1-3 August 1887   County Championship

Location: The Oval

On the first day 24,450 paid admission and, together with members, the crowd numbered about 27,000. This was a strong bid by Surrey to win the championship from Nottinghamshire, who had won for the previous three years. Winning the toss, Nottinghamshire scored 46 in the first hour and then Dixon was caught at backward point. With the score at 64 Gunn was caught at the wicket to loud cheers from the Surrey partisans. Shrewsbury was also caught at the wicket having been in for one-and-three-quarter hours for his 41. Lunch was taken with the score at 93. The crowd on the field delayed the restart until 3 p.m. With the eighth wicket falling at 143 it appeared that Nottinghamshire would post a low total. However, a bad miss at extra mid-off on 4 gave Richardson a life and, in company with his captain, 79 was added for the last wicket, Richardson completing an excellent fifty including seven fours.

On the second day about 20,000 people enjoyed a match of fluctuating character and most exciting cricket. The Nottinghamshire fielding was very bad with no fewer than five catches being missed. Sherwin had injured his hands so Gunn, probably the best outfielder in England at the time, took over the gloves. The third wicket fell at 76 with Shuter caught at slip off Richardson but, in his next over, Maurice Read was missed twice. He hadn't scored at this point and was then dropped for the third time by Richardson in the slips. Barnes moved to slip and promptly caught Henderson; 96 for 5. Lohmann joined Read and added 50 for the sixth wicket before being stumped. Beaumont was run out from long off by Lockwood, who was substituting for Sherwin. Read was caught at third man off a very bad hit. Bowley was missed by Gunn behind the wicket before scoring. Runs were accumulated from many overthrows. Brockwell was caught in the slips as one run was needed to avoid the follow-on. Wood, suffering with a bad hand, came in and quickly cut Sulley for four and the follow-on was prevented to great applause.

Although Nottinghamshire scored rapidly in their second innings wickets fell at regular short intervals. Daft and Dixon hit out freely but Lohmann came back on and bowled Dixon off stump. Walter Read was brought on at 120 with his 'lobs' and successfully took return catches from Flowers and Richardson. At the close of play Nottinghamshire were 184 for 9.

In front of a 12,000 crowd, the scene when Surrey beat Nottinghamshire was described in *The Times*

Maurice Read.

as probably the greatest county match ever played. Three days' exciting cricket saw the result in doubt until nearly the finish. Though Surrey won, Nottinghamshire may be said to have thrown the match away through dropped catches, but they still played with determination. After the early loss of Abel, Shuter and Key played admirable cricket. Key was dismissed with the score at 77 and Walter Read added a few runs. Barnes entered the attack and took 3 wickets in quick succession to leave Surrey needing a further 78 to win as Lohmann joined Maurice Read at the wicket. Some of the best cricket of the match was then played and too much praise could not be given to Read and Lohmann. Read was out with only 6 more runs needed and Wood was able to support Lohmann as the winning runs were achieved. The spectators were highly elated and there were scenes of excitement at The Oval such had not been seen for a long time. The overall paid attendance for the three days was a record 51,607.

SURREY v. NOTTINGHAMSHIRE

Played at The Oval on 1st, 2nd and 3rd August 1887 [3-day Match]   Toss: Nottinghamshire
Surrey won by 4 wickets

NOTTINGHAMSHIRE

Batsman	Dismissal	R	Dismissal 2	R
A. Shrewsbury	c Wood b Lohmann	41	c Bowley b Beaumont	5
J.A. Dixon	c W.W. Read b Abel	30	b Lohmann	46
W. Gunn	c Wood b Bowley	4	c J.M. Read b Beaumont	2
W. Barnes	c Shuter b Lohmann	43	b Abel	17
H.B. Daft	c Lohmann b Bowley	7	b Lohmann	40
W. Flowers	c W.W. Read b Lohmann	1	c & b W.W. Read	16
W. Attewell	c Wood b Beaumont	1	c Abel b Lohmann	0
F.J. Shacklock	c Lohmann b Beaumont	15	(9) c Abel b Bowley	15
H. Richardson	not out	54	(8) c & b W.W. Read	4
J. Sulley	b Bowley	11	run out	4
*#M. Sherwin	c & b W.W. Read	34	not out	10
Extras	b 3, lb 4	7	b 7, lb 1, w 1	9
Total	**(all out)**	**248**	**(all out)**	**168**

SURREY

Batsman	Dismissal	R	Dismissal 2	R
R. Abel	c Richardson b Barnes	2	c Sulley b Richardson	3
*J. Shuter	c Sulley b Richardson	44	b Barnes	53
K.J. Key	c Attewell b Barnes	0	c Sherwin b Sulley	38
W.W. Read	b Sulley	25	b Barnes	18
J.M. Read	c Shacklock b Sulley	40	c Richardson b Sulley	38
R. Henderson	c Barnes b Sulley	14	c Sherwin b Barnes	2
G.A. Lohmann	st Gunn b Attewell	17	not out	35
J. Beaumont	run out	4		
W. Brockwell	c Barnes b Sulley	4		
T. Bowley	b Attewell	36		
#H. Wood	not out	14	(8) not out	5
Extras	b 10, lb 1, w 1	12	b 11, lb 2	13
Total	**(all out)**	**212**	**(for 6 wickets)**	**205**

Bowling [4 balls per over]

SURREY	O	M	R	W	O	M	R	W
Bowley	46	20	72	3	10	4	15	1
Lohmann	61	38	59	3	35	18	46	3
Beaumont	31	10	61	2	18	7	50	2
Abel	22	13	20	1	16	8	21	1
W.W. Read	5.3	2	9	1	18	5	27	2
Henderson	6	2	9	0				
Brockwell	5	2	11	0				
J.M. Read	1	1	0	0				

NOTTINGHAMSHIRE	O	M	R	W	O	M	R	W
Barnes	19	3	51	2	29.2	10	56	3
Attewell	26.2	14	43	2	17	6	22	0
Sulley	36	15	66	4	29	15	40	2
Richardson	29	16	39	1	33	16	33	1
Flowers	1	0	1	0	11	4	16	0
Shacklock					10	3	20	0
Dixon					2	1	5	0

FALL OF WICKETS

	N	S	N	S
1st	47	14	31	7
2nd	64	16	35	77
3rd	80	76	56	118
4th	105	76	97	123
5th	110	96	130	127
6th	123	146	132	199
7th	143	152	136	–
8th	143	157	138	–
9th	169	168	143	–
10th	248	212	168	–

Umpires: C. Payne and J. Rowbotham

SURREY v. LANCASHIRE

Date: 2 August 1888

County Championship

Location: Old Trafford

The instances of a match being completed in one day are very rare. At the time, it was anticipated that the Lancashire eleven was the most likely team to lower the colours of the formidable Surrey team of 1888. Unfortunately, Lancashire were unable to secure the services of four notable amateurs, which considerably weakened their side.

Mr Hornby, the Lancashire captain, having won the toss decided to bat first. The weather was fine, but the ground, as it dried under the sunshine, was certainly all in favour of the bowlers, and going in first was undoubtedly an advantage. Some very remarkable bowling by Lohmann, however, deprived Lancashire of any benefit from winning the toss, and in an hour-and-a-half the home team had been dismissed for the small total of 35. Even this total would not have been reached but for a bad decision that gave Pilling a life before he had scored. As it was, Pilling's 10 was the only double-figure score on the side, and six of the eleven failed to make a run. Lohmann's figures were really extraordinary. He bowled 23 overs and 1 ball, of which 18 were maidens, for 13 runs and 8 wickets and of these 5 were clean bowled.

Surrey's innings did not open very well and, though Shuter made 17 in excellent style, the score was only 23 when the third wicket fell. With Shuter, Abel and Maurice Read all out, things did not look very good, but a determined stand by Walter Read and Key gave quite a new aspect to the game. The two amateurs added 58 runs while they were together, and their partnership did much to influence the result. Lohmann subsequently made 14 by free hitting, but no one stayed long with Read, who carried his bat for 49. Going in second wicket down, he was in while 101 runs were added and, considering the state of the ground, it was a display of very high merit. He did not seem to be troubled by the bowling at all, and his batting was marked by great judgment as well as freedom.

In a minority of 88, Lancashire began their second innings at 5 p.m. and, thanks to Sugg and Barlow, the total was 36 when the third batsman was dismissed. After this Lohmann and Beaumont bowled with irresistible effect and the ninth wicket fell for an addition of only 2 runs. Though just at the close Watson relieved the game by some vigorous hitting the end soon came and, when the tenth wicket fell at 63 Surrey were left with a decisive victory by an innings and 25 runs. Beaumont and Lohmann shared the 10 wickets equally, and the former had the better analysis, his 5 costing only 19 runs.

George Lohmann.

In the match altogether Lohmann took 13 wickets at an average of just under 4 runs, and of the 13 as many as 10 were bowled. It is worthy of remark that the time of actual play was about five hours, and during this period 30 wickets fell for an aggregate of 221 runs.

Nine years later Lohmann's fellow Surrey professional Robert Henderson recalled this famous day at Old Trafford: 'On the next morning the sun came out baking hot. George Lohmann and I walked down to the ground together and, after looking for a minute or two at the pitch, Lohmann said to me: "I'll bet you that this match is over by six o'clock tonight." And he was only wrong by quarter of an hour... I have never seen first-class batsmen so much at a loss... It was simply impossible to do anything with him.'

SURREY *v.* LANCASHIRE

Played at Old Trafford on 2nd August 1888 [3 day Match]   Toss: Lancashire
Surrey won by an innings and 25 runs

LANCASHIRE

*A.N. Hornby	b Lohmann	8	c Wood b Beaumont	3
R.G. Barlow	b Lohmann	8	b Beaumont	11
F.H. Sugg	lbw b Lohmann	0	b Lohmann	20
J. Briggs	c W.W. Read b Bowley	0	b Lohmann	2
S.M. Crosfield	b Lohmann	3	b Beaumont	1
G.R. Baker	b Lohmann	0	b Beaumont	0
D. Whittaker	c & b Lohmann	0	b Beaumont	0
F. Ward	b Lohmann	0	b Lohmann	1
G. Yates	c & b Bowley	3	b Lohmann	0
#R. Pilling	lbw b Lohmann	10	b Lohmann	1
A. Watson	not out	1	not out	18
Extras	b 2	2	lb 6	6
Total	**(all out)**	**35**	**(all out)**	**63**

SURREY

R. Abel	c Barlow b Briggs	4
*J. Shuter	b Watson	17
J.M. Read	b Watson	0
W.W. Read	not out	49
K.J. Key	lbw b Briggs	25
R. Henderson	b Briggs	0
G.A. Lohmann	c Crosfield b Barlow	14
#H. Wood	c Hornby b Briggs	0
M.P. Bowden	b Watson	6
J. Beaumont	c & b Watson	2
T. Bowley	st Pilling b Briggs	2
Extras	b 3, lb 1	4
Total	**(all out)**	**123**

Bowling [4 balls per over]

SURREY	O	M	R	W	O	M	R	W
Lohmann	23.1	18	13	8	21	10	38	5
Bowley	23	13	20	2	1	1	0	0
Beaumont					19	10	19	5

LANCASHIRE	O	M	R	W
Briggs	32.1	17	49	5
Barlow	17	5	37	1
Watson	21	13	20	4
Baker	6	1	13	0

FALL OF WICKETS

	L	S	L
1st	10	22	7
2nd	10	22	28
3rd	15	33	36
4th	21	80	37
5th	21	80	37
6th	21	?	37
7th	24	95	37
8th	24	108	37
9th	26	?	38
10th	35	123	63

Umpires: H. Holmes and J. Rowbotham

SURREY v. YORKSHIRE

Date: 20-22 August 1888   **County Championship**
Location: Bradford

Under the captaincy of John Shuter, Surrey were County Champions every year from 1888 to 1892 although the Championship was only recognised by all counties from 1890. George Lohmann was the leading wicket-taker for the county from 1885 to 1891.

Losing the toss, Yorkshire had the worst of luck and Surrey were able to claim a very easy victory. Despite the failure of Walter Read and John Shuter, Surrey succeeded in scoring 326 for the loss of 5 wickets on the first day. The merit of this performance rested with four batsmen, Abel, Bowden, Maurice Read and Key. Abel, who gave no chance in his score of 60, stayed until the total was 167, but the stand of the day was while Read and Key were partners. Both batsmen hit finely and the former's 109, which contained no chance till he had got 66, was an exceptionally good display of vigorous cricket that had followed a particular run of bad luck in earlier matches.

Owing to heavy rain during the night, due to the wet turf the bowlers were seen to such disadvantage that the not-out batsmen, Key and Lohmann, both scored fast. The latter, who was in only an hour and fifty minutes, hit in brilliant style, and both were out at the same total (417), Lohmann having added 57 while his partner was making 28. Key should have been stumped when he was on 7, but he hit well all round the wicket and altogether his 108 was deserving of high praise. Some loose fielding marked the close of the Surrey innings, and 38 were added by the last 3 wickets, of which Wood contributed 27 not out. Yorkshire had to bat on Tuesday afternoon under the double disadvantage of a drying wicket and bad light. When rain stopped play at 5.35 p.m. 7 of their wickets had fallen for only 79 runs.

As they were 354 runs behind, the Yorkshiremen followed on at 12.15 p.m., with small hope of being able to save the match. Ulyett's hitting gave a momentary interest to the game, and he was seen to the very best advantage in the attainment of his score of 51. When he was out the total was 89 for 4 wickets and, as no one afterwards made a lengthy stand, the end soon came, Surrey were left with a victory by an innings and 228 runs. Lohmann's bowling was again one of the principal factors in Surrey's success. Altogether he took 13 Yorkshire wickets for 119 runs. As he scored 80 in addition, the value of his all-round cricket to the side can be appreciated. His career lasted from 1884 to 1896, during which time he took 1,221 wickets for Surrey and accounted for 5 wickets in an innings on no less than 128 occasions. Although he was no more than medium-fast he had a repertoire that kept batsmen guessing. 'Owing to his naturally high delivery the ball described a pronounced curve and dropped rather sooner than the batsmen expected. He was the perfect master of the whole art of varying his pace,' wrote C.B. Fry.

The Surrey team, 1891. From left to right, back row: G.A. Lohmann, J.M. Read, W.W. Read, H. Wood. Seated: W.H. Lockwood, K.J. Key, J. Shuter, R. Abel, W. Brockwell. Front row: R. Henderson, J.W. Sharpe.

SURREY *v.* YORKSHIRE

Played at Bradford on 20th, 21st and 22nd August 1888 [3-day Match] Toss: Surrey
Surrey won by an innings and 228 runs

SURREY

*J. Shuter	c Lee b Preston	6
R. Abel	c Middlebrook b Wade	60
M.P. Bowden	b Middlebrook	34
W.W. Read	b Middlebrook	1
J.M. Read	b Preston	109
K.J. Key	b Wainwright	108
G.A. Lohmann	c Lee b Ulyett	80
R. Henderson	b Middlebrook	6
#H. Wood	not out	27
J. Beaumont	b Middlebrook	2
T. Bowley	c Wade b Peel	3
Extras	b 18, w 1	19
Total	**(all out)**	**455**

YORKSHIRE

G. Ulyett	c J.M. Read b Lohmann	5	b Bowley	51
L. Hall	lbw b Lohmann	16	b Lohmann	9
F. Lee	c Henderson b Lohmann	18	c W.W. Read b Bowley	17
E.T. Hirst	c Wood b Lohmann	8	b Lohmann	0
R. Peel	c W.W. Read b Bowley	15	b Beaumont	17
J.M. Preston	b Lohmann	4	b Lohmann	1
E. Wainwright	c W.W. Read b Henderson	4	b Lohmann	8
*Lord Hawke	b Lohmann	3	b Beaumont	6
#A. Wormald	b Bowley	17	b Lohmann	0
S. Wade	b Lohmann	5	b Lohmann	4
W. Middlebrook	not out	1	not out	0
Extras	b 2, lb 3	5	b 9, lb 4	13
Total	**(all out)**	**101**	**(all out)**	**126**

Bowling [4 balls per over]

YORKSHIRE	O	M	R	W
Peel	73.2	31	104	1
Preston	38	13	88	2
Middlebrook	49	21	88	4
Wade	27	6	54	1
Wainwright	19	5	34	1
Ulyett	26	16	40	1
Hall	12	3	28	0

SURREY	O	M	R	W	O	M	R	W
Lohmann	50	22	59	7	47.1	18	60	6
Beaumont	29	19	25	0	17	13	7	2
Henderson	11	5	11	1				
Bowley	9	8	1	2	37	28	32	2
Abel					7	3	14	0

FALL OF WICKETS

	S	Y	Y
1st	14	10	31
2nd	64	40	78
3rd	66	45	81
4th	169	54	89
5th	289	58	90
6th	417	67	104
7th	417	72	119
8th	448	82	120
9th	450	99	?
10th	455	101	126

Umpires: J. Breedon and F.J. Whatmough

Surrey v. Yorkshire

Date: 26-27 August 1889   **County Championship**
Location: The Oval

Surrey beat Yorkshire after a very even game with only 2 wickets to spare. The ground was slow at the outset and though it was playing better at the finish, when Surrey had to make the runs it was never really easy.

Lord Hawke winning the toss, Surrey had to take the field. Not for long, however, as though Ulyett and Hall made a good start, Beaumont's bowling proved so effective that Yorkshire only reached 138. It was only a plucky stand by Moorhouse and Wade, who added 59 for the eighth wicket, that enabled them to do so well, and Moorhouse played with great confidence for his 47 not out. In catching Lord Hawke in the long field, Maurice Read hurt his right hand so badly that he was unable to field, and he was only able to go in last to bat using only one hand. Surrey in their turn did badly, being dismissed for 114 and, had the fielding been up to the mark, they would have done much worse as several catches were missed. Hunter's wicketkeeping, though, was a redeeming feature.

When play began on Tuesday Yorkshire were 30 on with all their wickets in hand. Wade and Ulyett were soon dismissed but Lee and Hall advanced the score to 73. Lohmann came on again at 96 and the game underwent a great change, for the Yorkshire innings only reached 141. Lord Hawke, whose hand had been injured by Beaumont's bowling on the first day, was unable to bat. Surrey, wanting 166 to win, went in just after 3 p.m. on Tuesday, so that to finish that evening the runs had to be obtained in just under three-and-a-quarter hours. A very bad start was made, as at 17 Abel was caught at mid-off, at 20 Mr Shuter was bowled, at 25 Wainwright dismissed Mr Read and 18 runs later the same player bowled Lohmann. With four of the best batsmen out for 43, and Maurice Read injured, Surrey's chances were, apparently, very slight. Key found a useful partner in Henderson, and while they were together hopes rose fast. After adding 35 Key was cleverly thrown out by Whitehead in trying to make a second run.

This piece of luck turned the scale once more against Surrey, and when Wainwright, after getting rid of Lockwood at 95, bowled Wood at 107, Yorkshire seemed again to have the game in hand. With 59 still wanted, and practically only 2 wickets to fall, Sharpe came in to join Henderson. He batted with such judgment and pluck that 29 were added before he was bowled for a most deserving and well-played

John Beaumont.

14. Beaumont now faced Henderson, who had been playing all the bowlers carefully and well.

At 6.15 p.m., the time for drawing stumps, 26 were still wanted to win, but the captains agreed to go on for another half-hour to finish that night. In spite of several changes of bowling and fine all-round fielding runs came slowly, the excitement increasing as Surrey got within measurable distance of victory. At 6.45 p.m. the score was only 152, but in spite of the fading light it was agreed to finish, and just before 7 p.m. Henderson made the winning hit, Surrey thus securing the victory after a brilliant finish with 2 wickets to spare. There was a scene of great excitement, and Henderson, who was in two-and-three-quarter hours for his 59, was heartily cheered. A game has rarely been finished under such conditions, as for some twenty minutes before the close the gas lamps in the streets around The Oval were being lit. Consequently, this match has since been known as the 'Gaslight Match'.

SURREY v. YORKSHIRE

Played at The Oval on 26th and 27th August 1889 [3-day Match]   Toss: Yorkshire
Surrey won by 2 wickets

YORKSHIRE

G. Ulyett	c Shuter b Beaumont	22	[3] b Lohmann		2
L. Hall	b Beaumont	14	b Lohmann		33
F. Lee	b Beaumont	12	[4] b Lockwood		32
R. Peel	c Henderson b Beaumont	2	[5] b Lohmann		22
E. Wainwright	b Beaumont	7	[6] b Lohmann		5
*Lord Hawke	c J.M. Read b Lohmann	7	absent hurt		
J.T. Brown	c Wood b Beaumont	3	c Wood b Beaumont		10
S. Wade	b Sharpe	23	[1] c W.W. Read b Sharpe		3
R. Moorhouse	not out	47	[8] c Wood b Beaumont		17
L. Whitehead	b Sharpe	0	[9] b Lohmann		2
#D. Hunter	b Sharpe	0	[10] not out		1
Extras	lb 1	1	b 12, lb 1, nb 1		14
Total	**(all out)**	**138**	**(all out)**		**141**

SURREY

R. Abel	c Whitehead b Peel	5	c Wainwright b Peel		4
*J. Shuter	b Wainwright	24	b Peel		11
K.J. Key	c Lee b Peel	6	run out		33
W.W. Read	st Hunter b Peel	14	b Wainwright		4
G.A. Lohmann	st Hunter b Peel	6	b Wainwright		1
R. Henderson	b Whitehead	14	not out		59
W.H. Lockwood	st Hunter b Peel	6	b Wainwright		7
#H. Wood	c Wainwright b Whitehead	21	b Wainwright		8
J.W. Sharpe	b Whitehead	0	b Ulyett		14
J. Beaumont	c Hunter b Whitehead	2	not out		8
J.M. Read	not out	4			
Extras	b 3, lb 2	5	b 14, lb 3		17
Total	**(all out)**	**114**	**(for 8 wickets)**		**166**

Bowling [5 balls per over]

SURREY	O	M	R	W	O	M	R	W
Beaumont	30	15	46	6	22.2	15	25	2
Lohmann	29	8	68	1	33	14	53	5
Sharpe	4.3	2	7	3	17	8	28	1
W.W. Read	1	0	4	0	3	0	9	0
Abel	2	0	12	0				
Lockwood					15	9	12	1

YORKSHIRE	O	M	R	W	O	M	R	W
Peel	29	11	50	5	42	16	51	2
Wainwright	20	6	46	1	36	15	43	4
Whitehead	8.3	3	13	4	14	6	27	0
Wade					15	8	13	0
Ulyett					9.3	4	15	1

FALL OF WICKETS

	Y	S	Y	S
1st	34	11	26	17
2nd	40	37	28	20
3rd	52	43	73	25
4th	55	50	97	43
5th	58	59	109	77
6th	66	85	118	97
7th	71	85	124	105
8th	130	97	129	136
9th	130	105	141	—
10th	138	114	—	—

Umpires: R.P. Carpenter and R.A. Thoms

Surrey v. Lancashire

Date: 16-18 August 1894   **County Championship**
Location: The Oval

Rain delayed the start of play until the Friday morning, the second scheduled day. The wicket never had the chance to dry out. Surrey won the toss but gained no advantage in batting first and later in the day Lancashire found the wicket faster and run-getting more easy. Briggs made the ball do a great deal and Surrey lost their first 4 wickets for 28. Hayward and Street were the first pair to make a stand, and when the former, who had been in for over an hour scoring 15, was caught the total was 53 with half the side out. Street batted with confidence and made 48 out of the last 69 runs in the Surrey total. His judicious and plucky cricket merited the highest praise. He ought to have been caught in the long field when he had made 23, but otherwise the Lancashire fielding was all round distinctly above the average. The whole Surrey innings of 97 lasted just two-and-a-half hours with Briggs taking 7 wickets for 46.

Though McLaren and Ward put on the first 20 runs in less than a quarter of an hour, Lockwood and Richardson exploited the conditions to reduce Lancashire to 46 for 6. Tindall and Tinsey showed great nerve and judgement during an invaluable partnership of 37 for the seventh wicket, which enabled Lancashire to take a first innings lead of 50, the last 4 wickets adding no less than 101 runs. Wood was in great form for Surrey behind the stumps, catching four while standing back and stumping one. With forty minutes' play left in the day in light that, at times, was a little trying, Surrey faired very badly and lost the 4 wickets of Lockwood, Abel, Hayward and Brockwell.

Being still 9 runs behind at the start of play on Saturday the chances of the home team saving the match were very small. Solid cricket by Ayres and Wood steadied the ship and then Read carried his bat for 33. With Street he added 28 for the seventh wicket but the last 3 wickets fell for a mere 9 runs. Briggs finished with a match analysis of 13 for 93. With Lancashire needing just 75 to win Surrey were soon in with a chance as in the first over Lockwood bowled both Ward and Sugg. Heavy rain stopped play at

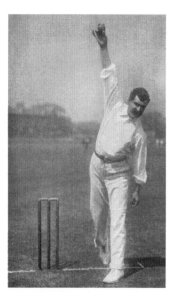

Tom Richardson.

1.45 p.m. but, on the resumption, Lockwood and Richardson reduced Lancashire to 9 for 5. A fine catch by Abel at short slip accounted for McLaren and then caught Tindall off a skier to leave the score 26 for 7. A victory for Surrey then seemed a mere matter of time, as 49 were still wanted with 3 wickets in hand. At the crisis, however, Tinsley and Smith then played some very fine cricket to add 30 valuable runs but Hayward was brought back for one over and had Smith caught at cover point.

With only 10 runs now needed 8 of them came very quickly but Bardswell was then caught at the wicket by Wood, standing back. Tinsley was dropped in the slips but with the ball being stopped before it reached the boundary it meant that the scores were then level. Mold was caught by Wood, still standing back, and the match was tied. Lockwood had nearly pulled off a remarkable victory with his 6 wickets in the second innings. There was naturally great excitement at the finish, and it was some time before the enthusiasm of the spectators subsided. In their history Surrey have been involved in only 6 tied matches out of the 3,429 played.

SURREY v. LANCASHIRE

Played at The Oval on 16th, 17th and 18th August 1894 [3-day Match]   Toss: Surrey
Match tied

SURREY

Batsman	Dismissal 1	R	Dismissal 2	R
R. Abel	c Paul b Briggs	5	b Mold	13
W.H. Lockwood	c Bardswell b Briggs	7	c Paul b Mold	13
T.W. Hayward	c Bardswell b Briggs	16	c Bardswell b Briggs	0
W. Brockwell	b Briggs	1	c Bardswell b Briggs	5
W.W. Read	c Ward b Briggs	8	(7) not out	33
A.E. Street	b Mold	48	(8) c Baker b Mold	12
G.W. Ayres	st Smith b Briggs	2	(6) c MacLaren b Bardswell	23
*K.J. Key	c Smith b Mold	1	(9) st Smith b Briggs	7
F.E. Smith	c Mold b Briggs	0	(10) b Briggs	0
T. Richardson	b Mold	6	(11) c & b Briggs	2
#H. Wood	not out	2	(5) c Bardswell b Briggs	10
Extras	lb 1	1	b 2, lb 4	6
Total	**(all out)**	**97**	**(all out)**	**124**

LANCASHIRE

Batsman	Dismissal 1	R	Dismissal 2	R
*A.C. McLaren	c Wood b Richardson	10	c Abel b Lockwood	6
A. Ward	b Lockwood	15	b Lockwood	0
F.H. Sugg	c Read b Richardson	8	b Lockwood	0
A.G. Paul	c Wood b Richardson	5	b Richardson	3
J. Briggs	c Wood b Lockwood	4	b Lockwood	1
G.R. Baker	b Lockwood	0	b Richardson	0
S.M. Tindall	c & b Hayward	49	c Abel b Lockwood	11
A. Tinsley	st Wood b Smith	19	not out	19
#C. Smith	c Wood b Richardson	20	c Smith b Hayward	21
G.R. Bardswell	c Ayres b Richardson	12	c Wood b Richardson	4
A.W. Mold	not out	0	c Wood b Lockwood	0
Extras	lb 5	5	b 4, lb 5	9
Total	**(all out)**	**147**	**(all out)**	**74**

Bowling [5 balls per over]

LANCASHIRE	O	M	R	W	O	M	R	W
Briggs	34	16	46	7	28.4	11	47	6
Mold	24.1	14	34	3	22	8	61	3
Bardswell	9	5	16	0	6	3	10	1

SURREY	O	M	R	W	O	M	R	W
Richardson	22.3	9	52	5	13	3	26	3
Lockwood	17	3	48	3	14	4	30	6
Smith	4	1	11	1				
Abel	2	0	15	0				
Hayward	5	1	16	1	1	0	9	1

FALL OF WICKETS

	S	L	S	L
1st	5	20	21	2
2nd	12	34	26	2
3rd	14	36	32	5
4th	28	40	34	5
5th	53	40	63	9
6th	73	46	77	25
7th	74	83	105	26
8th	87	125	118	62
9th	94	142	118	73
10th	97	147	124	74

Umpires: H. Draper and E. Henty

SURREY v. LEICESTERSHIRE

Date: 7-9 June 1906   County Championship
Location: Leicester

Surrey, thanks to Hayward and Hobbs, commenced so well in this match that 178 runs were made before the first wicket fell. Hobbs made 73 in 140 minutes but was missed when he was 56. The feature of the first innings, however, was the batting of Hayward, who made 50 out of 86 in seventy-five minutes, 100 in two-and-a-quarter hours and, in all, 143 out of 230 in 170 minutes. He was let off when he had made 50 – an expensive mistake. Baker and Crawford put on 65 for the fourth wicket in fifty minutes, and later Dalmeny, chiefly by a series of fine drives, made 66 in forty-five minutes. After five hours, the innings closed for 425 and, by the time stumps were drawn, the home side had responded with 21 without loss.

On Friday De Trafford was sent back at 40 but Wood, who was missed when 10, reached 50 out of 117 in ninety minutes, and then batted another twenty minutes without augmenting his score. With King he added 42 for the second wicket and with Crawford 48 for the third. V.F.S.Crawford made 73 out of 117 obtained while in, reaching 50 out of 85 in an hour. With Knight, he put on 39 for the fourth wicket in thirty-five minutes. During the afternoon the Surrey fielding was frequently at fault, Crawford and Knight each being missed twice, Wood and King once each. Knight played a very valuable innings, scoring 72 in ninety minutes and with Coe put on 75 for the fifth wicket in forty-five minutes. In the absence of Whitehead, with an injured hand, the innings closed at the fall of the ninth wicket, at 331. With a lead of 94, Surrey lost Hobbs at 25, and so greatly did the bowlers obtain the upper hand that the score was only 106 when the sixth wicket went down. Hayward, who was missed when on 2, claimed 72 of the 132 runs scored by the close of play.

On Saturday Hayward quickly reached three figures, thereby setting up a special record by scoring four separate hundreds in a week for a total of 512 runs, being dismissed three times. His earlier centuries, 144 not out and 100, were against Nottinghamshire at Trent Bridge, in a match won by Surrey by 5 wickets. Hayward had made these four scores in succession, and, better still, not in a single case did he get a run that was not wanted. Lees rendered great service to the side by helping to add 103 for the seventh wicket in ninety minutes. The innings closed for 218, and Leicestershire were set 313 to get to win on a somewhat worn wicket. De Trafford was out without scoring and, at the end of an hour, 4 wickets were down for 50. Knight and Coe then put on 64 together for the fifth in forty minutes, the latter, who was twice missed, scoring 76 in 100 minutes and hitting seven fours. Surrey went on to win by 110 runs.

This match unusually featured brothers playing on opposite sides. V.F.S. Crawford was born in Leicester but went to school at Whitgift in Croydon. He played for Surrey from 1896 to 1902, reaching 1,000 runs in a season five times. In 1903 he was appointed secretary to Leicestershire CCC and therefore moved back to his native county. In 1910 he emigrated to Ceylon, becoming a tea-planter, but returned to serve in the First World War. J.N. Crawford played for Surrey from 1904 to 1909 but, following a quarrel with the Club, emigrated to Australia. He returned in 1914 to serve in the First World War and played again for Surrey from 1919 to 1921.

Tom Hayward.

SURREY v. LEICESTERSHIRE

Played at Aylestone Road, Leicester on 7th, 8th and 9th June 1906 [3-day Match]   Toss: Surrey
Surrey won by 110 runs

SURREY

T.W. Hayward	c Coe b King	143	c Coe b Jayes	125
J.B. Hobbs	hit wkt b Coe	73	b Jayes	14
E.G. Hayes	c Whiteside b Jayes	0	c Whiteside b Gill	26
A. Baker	c Odell b Jayes	47	c Whiteside b Gill	0
J.N. Crawford	c Whiteside b Odell	30	run out	0
*Lord Dalmeny	c Odell b Coe	66	c Jayes b Odell	9
J.H. Moulder	c Knight b Odell	6	b Odell	0
W.S. Lees	c Crawford b Coe	14	c Crawford b Jayes	34
#H. Strudwick	c Coe b Gill	29	c & b Jayes	0
W.C. Smith	c & b Gill	4	not out	1
N.A. Knox	not out	8	c Wood b Coe	4
Extras	b 2, lb 2, w 1	5	b 4, lb 1	5
Total	**(all out)**	**425**	**(all out)**	**218**

LEICESTERSHIRE

*C.E. deTrafford	c Strudwick b Knox	18	c Smith b Lees	0
C.J.B. Wood	b Hayes	50	c Hayes b Knox	7
J.H. King	c Dalmeny b Knox	25	c Hayes b Knox	21
V.F.S. Crawford	c Baker b Smith	73	c Hayes b Knox	7
A.E. Knight	c Hayward b Lees	72	c Hayward b Crawford	37
S. Coe	c Moulder b Knox	34	c Moulder b Knox	76
T. Jayes	c Hayes b Lees	12	c & b Crawford	11
W.W. Odell	not out	22	c & b Hayes	14
G.C. Gill	lbw b Moulder	14	not out	19
#J.P. Whiteside	b Crawford	0	b Crawford	1
H. Whitehead	absent hurt		absent hurt	
Extras	b 6, lb 3, w 2	11	b 7, w 2	9
Total	**(all out)**	**331**	**(all out)**	**202**

Bowling [6 balls per over]

LEICESTERSHIRE	O	M	R	W	O	M	R	W
Gill	22.3	0	102	0	18	5	57	2
Odell	24	5	103	2	15	3	41	2
Coe	20	2	68	3	14.2	1	48	1
Jayes	24	1	117	2	19	3	67	4
King	12	6	22	1				
Crawford	2	0	8	0				

SURREY	O	M	R	W	O	M	R	W
Lees	28	6	83	2	18	5	34	1
Knox	27	2	152	3	18	1	85	4
Crawford	14.4	5	42	1	14.5	1	68	3
Hayes	5	0	22	1	2	0	6	1
Smith	2	0	18	1				
Moulder	1	0	3	1				

FALL OF WICKETS

	S	L	S	L
1st	177	40	25	0
2nd	178	82	86	20
3rd	230	130	86	36
4th	295	199	86	50
5th	313	274	102	114
6th	349	290	106	138
7th	379	301	209	173
8th	408	328	213	197
9th	409	331	213	202
10th	425	–	218	–

Umpires: F.W. Marlow and A. Millward

SURREY v. NORTHAMPTONSHIRE

Date: 25-27 May 1911   **County Championship**
Location: Northampton

Surrey defeated Northamptonshire at Northampton on the last day by 1 wicket after a very exciting finish. Although Surrey, on the first day, dismissed the home side for 239 and then equalled that total with 7 wickets in hand, they had to struggle severely at the end to pull off the match. In Northamptonshire's first innings, Seymour and Denton made 95 for the first wicket and Waldon and Haywood 70 for the sixth but the others did little against Walter Lees, who took 7 wickets. Though perhaps never quite in the front rank of bowlers, being very good without being great, Walter Lees had a long and distinguished career playing for Surrey from 1896 to 1911.

It was by consistent batting that Surrey were so well positioned by the end of the day. Goatly, Hayes and Ducat helped Hobbs to make 72, 77 and 59 for the first 3 wickets respectively. The last named scored 92 by free cricket in two hours, giving no chance and hitting a dozen fours. Ducat compiled an innings of 60.

Heavy rain prevented any play on the second day but the third day opened with bright sunshine, which rendered the wicket exceedingly difficult. Surrey added only 51 runs to their score of 239 for 3 wickets, with only Rushby and Lees reaching double figures in a last-wicket stand of 30. William East bowled well to take 4 wickets and at one time had taken 3 wickets for 1 run

Northamptonshire made 130, which, under the conditions that prevailed, was a useful score. 'Razor' Smith bowled with marked effect on a pitch that was well suited to him and took 7 wickets for 62 runs. Smith was another cricketer who served Surrey well, playing from 1900 to 1914 and taking 1,036 wickets in all. Because he suffered with a frail physique and a weak heart he rarely played through a full season but when equal to the strain of much work, he seldom failed.

William 'Razor' Smith.

Surrey were left with 80 runs to get to win on a ruined pitch, but the wicket was then at its worst and the winning hit was not made until the last pair were together. Fifty were made with only 4 wickets, but at 59 Harrison fell to a capital return catch by Sydney Smith, and then an exciting struggle began. Spring was out at 60, and with 3 added Hobbs was run out through a brilliant piece of fielding by Walden. Sydney Smith bowled Strudwick 3 runs later, and with eight men out Surrey still required 14 to win. 'Razor' Smith and Rushby added 10 runs before Smith was bowled attempting a big hit. When Lees, the last man, went in Surrey required 4 more runs. Three singles made the game a tie, and then Rushby turned a ball from Seymour to leg and won the match.

SURREY _v._ NORTHAMPTONSHIRE

Played at Northampton on 25th, 26th and 27th May 1911 [3-day Match]   Toss: Not known
Surrey won by 1 wicket

NORTHAMPTONSHIRE

W.H. Denton	b Smith	26	not out		13
J. Seymour	c Harrison b Lees	57	c Rushby b Smith		3
W. East	b Smith	4	st Strudwick b Smith		13
S.G. Smith	c Hayes b Lees	0	b Smith		25
*G.A.T. Vials	b Lees	25	c Harrison b Smith		15
R.A. Haywood	c Smith b Lees	48	b Smith		0
F.I. Walden	not out	50	b Smith		9
J.N. Beasley	c Harrison b Hayes	2	c & b Smith		13
J.S. Denton	b Lees	0	c & b Rushby		7
E. Freeman	b Lees	1	b Bird		5
#W.A. Buswell	c Hayes b Lees	9	c & b Bird		11
Extras	b 14, lb 3	17	b 12, lb 4		16
Total	**(all out)**	**239**	**(all out)**		**130**

SURREY

J.B. Hobbs	c Buswell b J.S. Denton	92	run out		39
E.G. Goatly	c East b Seymour	42	lbw b Smith		3
E.G. Hayes	c Seymour b Smith	38	c Walden b Smith		10
A. Ducat	c J.S. Denton b East	60	c & b Smith		1
H.S. Harrison	run out	3	c & b Seymour		2
*M.C. Bird	c Seymour b East	3	run out		0
W.A. Spring	c Seymour b East	1	lbw b Smith		1
W.C. Smith	c Vials b Seymour	13	b Seymour		7
#H. Strudwick	c Seymour b East	3	b Smith		3
T. Rushby	b Smith	14	not out		8
W.S. Lees	not out	14	not out		2
Extras	b 3, lb 1, nb 3	7	b 3, lb 1		4
Total	**(all out)**	**290**	**(for 9 wickets)**		**80**

Bowling

SURREY	O	M	R	W	O	M	R	W
Lees	28.5	5	86	7				
Rushby	16	2	63	0	16	4	38	1
Smith	12	2	45	2	24	4	62	7
Hayes	8	0	28	1				
Bird					7.2	2	14	2

NORTHAMPTONSHIRE	O	M	R	W	O	M	R	W
East	31	10	84	4	8	3	23	0
Smith	24.5	3	76	2	17	6	25	5
Seymour	16	5	41	2	9.2	1	28	2
Freeman	4	0	18	0				
Haywood	7	1	23	0				
J.S. Denton	4	0	41	1				

FALL OF WICKETS

	N	S	N	S
1st	95	72	9	13
2nd	97	149	22	33
3rd	99	208	22	41
4th	103	241	58	47
5th	125	244	63	59
6th	195	245	75	60
7th	208	246	81	63
8th	215	252	113	66
9th	227	260	124	76
10th	239	290	130	–

Umpires: W. Flowers and F. Parris

SURREY v. YORKSHIRE

Date: 13-15 August 1914   **County Championship**
Location: Lord's

With the outbreak of the First World War on 4 August, The Oval was requisitioned by the Government, but first-class cricket continued. Hobbs, whose benefit match against Kent was due to be played the following week, was given the option by the Surrey committee of postponing his benefit until after the war or of having the match transferred to Lord's, where Surrey were to play the matches against Kent and Yorkshire as The Oval was not available. Hobbs chose to have his benefit match at Lord's, but it was something of a disaster as Kent were beaten in two days. The takings were poor, and a restricted collection brought in much less than it would have done at The Oval. Surrey offered to discount it as a benefit, retaining the gate money, keeping the subscription list open and restaging the match after the war. Hobbs accepted this generous offer.

On the first day of the Yorkshire match, Hayward and Hobbs opened with a stand of 290 and the first three batsmen scored centuries. Hobbs went on to score a double-century; he was to score ten innings over 200 for Surrey in his career with his highest score of all, 316 not out, also at Lord's in 1926. Lord's can be said to be a favourite ground for Hobbs as in 57 matches there he had 91 innings, scored 4,942 runs with sixteen centuries and twenty-four fifties to average 60.26.

Hayes was the third centurion and Surrey were able to declare on 549 for 6, and this was the third score of over 500 made by Surrey within a fortnight. Yorkshire were dismissed for 204 in rather less than four hours. Hitch began Surrey's good work in the field, taking 5 wickets. Abel, Rushby and Fender all bowled well and the fielding was brilliant. Over 5,000 people watched the second day's play and in the last three-quarters of an hour Yorkshire lost Oldroyd's wicket for 33.

On the last day Wilson and Denton added 93 for the second wicket. Wilson batted two hours and fifty minutes for his 95. Surrey steadily worked through the Yorkshire batting with Hitch, Rushby and Fender sharing the wickets and six of the dismissals being clean bowled. At one time during the afternoon it seemed as if rain would help Yorkshire in their desperate effort to save the game, but the last 4 wickets fell for 15 runs after the 300 went up. When this collapse was started by Rushby, Yorkshire, with four men to be dismissed, had reduced the arrears to 45. Stumps were to be drawn in less than an hour-and-a-half. Fortunately for Surrey, Fender perservered with his many bowling changes and Rushby and Hitch quickly brought the match to an end.

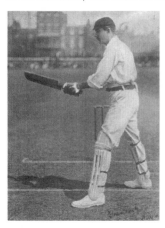
Ernie Hayes.

Later in the season The Oval was returned to the Club by the military authorities in time for the match against Gloucestershire who, owing to enlistments, could field only ten men. The Surrey committee, at a special meeting, decided to cancel the last two matches of the season. Popular feeling against continuing first-class cricket while a war was raging was beginning to run high. Surrey had a clear lead at the top of the Championship table but, as they had cancelled the last two matches, some people argued that they had forfeited the right to be champions and that the title should remain in abeyance for a year. This view received no official support and, at a meeting of the MCC committee in November 1914, a motion was passed that Surrey should be declared champions.

SURREY *v.* YORKSHIRE

Played at Lord's on 13th, 14th and 15th August 1914 [3-day Match]   Toss: Not known
Surrey won by an innings and 30 runs

SURREY

T.W. Hayward	c Wilson b Rhodes	116
J.B. Hobbs	st Dolphin b Drake	202
E.G. Hayes	c Dolphin b Kilner	134
D.J. Knight	c & b Oldroyd	21
J.W. Hitch	run out	16
A. Ducat	not out	34
*P.G.H. Fender	b Rhodes	5
H.S. Harrison		
W.J. Abel		
#H. Strudwick		
T. Rushby		
Extras	b 10, lb 9, nb 2	21
Total	**(for 6 wickets declared)**	**549**

YORKSHIRE

B.B. Wilson	c Strudwick b Hitch	4	c & b Rushby	95
E. Oldroyd	b Hitch	25	b Rushby	16
D. Denton	c Harrison b Hitch	44	c Hayward b Fender	52
R. Kilner	c Abel b Rushby	5	b Hitch	54
W. Rhodes	b Fender	29	b Hitch	2
G.H. Hirst	c Ducat b Hitch	39	b Fender	13
P. Holmes	lbw b Abel	5	b Hitch	27
A. Drake	st Strudwick b Abel	10	c Fender b Rushby	28
T.J.D. Birtles	not out	22	b Hitch	3
M.W. Booth	b Hitch	2	c Ducat b Rushby	1
#A. Dolphin	b Abel	12	not out	1
Extras	b 4, nb 3	7	b 14, lb 3, nb 4, w 2	23
Total	**(all out)**	**204**	**(all out)**	**315**

Bowling

YORKSHIRE	O	M	R	W
Booth	32	3	118	0
Drake	32	2	119	1
Hirst	16	1	61	0
Rhodes	38.5	6	134	2
Kilner	19	3	59	1
Oldroyd	7	0	37	1

SURREY	O	M	R	W	O	M	R	W
Hitch	26	9	64	5	26	8	66	4
Rushby	21	6	56	1	20	6	30	4
Fender	13	5	30	1	27	10	94	2
Abel	12	1	47	3	14	1	61	0
Hayes					10	2	35	0
Hobbs					3	1	6	0

FALL OF WICKETS

	S	Y	Y
1st	290	24	31
2nd	349	55	123
3rd	421	64	200
4th	467	105	213
5th	544	126	235
6th	549	145	249
7th	–	161	301
8th	–	171	309
9th	–	179	310
10th	–	204	315

Umpires: H.R. Butt and F. Parris

SURREY v. KENT

Date: 18-19 August 1919   County Championship

Location: The Oval

In 1919 County Championship matches were played over only two days. There was a crowd of about 18,000 at The Oval on the first day for the benefit match of Jack Hobbs. Kent stood at the head of the Championship and Surrey, strengthened by the return of J.N. Crawford, had a heavy defeat at Blackheath to avenge.

On the first day Kent, in spite of an excellent start, were all out for a very modest score and Surrey had time in which to get within 40 runs of their opponents with 6 wickets still in hand. Humphreys and Hardinge made a good start by putting on 68 for the Kent first wicket. Hardinge managed to divert a few loose ones from Hitch through the slips and made some hard hits to the off, but then he found it difficult to get the ball past the combination of Knight, Hobbs and Hitch, all standing deep. Humphrey's preference for leg strokes proved to be the undoing of Hardinge, who was called for a rather short run and just failed to beat a smart return finely gathered by Strudwick. Hitch, in the first over of his second spell, caused Seymour to play the ball onto his wicket. Woolley had a flattering reception when he went in, and he quickly showed the master hand by turning a ball from Hitch for four and by making a series of typical forcing strokes off his legs. Few batsmen can make defence so interesting to watch as Woolley; some of his back strokes kept the fieldsmen as busy as many other players' hardest drives would have done. Humphreys, meanwhile, had raised his own score to 58 when he fell, at last, to one of several rather lame strokes into the slips.

One over from Hitch cost 8 runs and the next over from Rushby cost a further 9 runs, so that Woolley doubled his score in 2 overs. This did not prevent a bad time for the side in general, however, for Hedges was bowled by Hitch for 1 in the last over before lunch, and directly afterwards Rushby found his best form, hitting the wickets of Hubble and Wood for the addition of only 1 run. Half the Kent side were therefore out for 131 but Troughton showed a bold front and made some nice drives, but he tried to lift the ball over mid-off once too often and was caught by Rushby. Johnstone's easy style promised better things and when Woolley was missed low down in the slips off Crawford just before he reached 50 an entire change of luck seemed quite possible. However, Woolley was then bowled by Crawford for 55. His innings cannot be judged in terms of runs alone; his judgment was perfect, and it is not too much to say that he saved Kent from a collapse that would have required a lot of explaining away. Fairservice and Freeman made a few runs but Freeman was then run out being stranded in the middle of the pitch.

Hobbs and Knight opened for Surrey and Hobbs played very freely. He was dropped in the gully but 7 runs later was caught and bowled. After Knight was out, Sandham helped Ducat to take the score to 78 but it was left to Harrison and Ducat to add a further 78 runs. Ducat was out shortly before the close but Harrison and Crawford survived in rather poor light to leave Surrey at 178 for 4 at the end of the first day.

On the second day Surrey had to work hard to gain a lead of 90. Crawford added 18 to his overnight score by means of some excellent pulls and drives before he was finely caught by Hedges. Peach then helped Harrison to pass the Kent score, but Freeman came on again at 234 and bowled Peach for a 17 that included several nice strokes. Harrison continued to play the part of pivotal man, and he was content to keep the side together while Hitch engaged in some rather uncertain slogging. Harrison's invaluable innings came to an end after 160 minutes' sound defensive batting. The score was 284 for 7 when Lockton

Above left: Andrew Ducat.

Above right: Jack Crawford.

joined Hitch, who was playing the bowling as it deserved to be played, and 42 very useful runs were the result. Lockton sent up the 300 with a powerful straight hit, but a few runs later Hitch was surprised by the pace of a ball from Fairservice, and Lockton himself was well caught in front of the pavilion in trying to hit another six, again at the expense of Woolley. Rushby soon found the bowling too much for him, and the innings closed abruptly for a total of 308.

Kent could hardly have made a worse start to a critical second innings, for they lost Humphreys and Seymour in Hitch's second over with only 3 runs scored. Humphreys was out to a remarkable catch by Knight, who held a hard cut with both hands as it was about to pass just over his head. Hitch was bowling his fastest in a very dull light and, 3 balls later, Seymour lost sight of one and was bowled for his second duck of the match. Kent were then in the doldrums for a long time and, just when it seemed as though they might be extricated by Hardinge and Woolley, the last-named hit a catch to Hobbs at cover-point, off the bowling of Rushby. Hedges was caught at the wicket for 12 off Rushby's bowling and, five minutes later, Hardinge suffered precisely the same fate. Half the side were then out for 74 and 16 runs were still wanted to equal Surrey's first innings. A long stand by Hubble and Colonel Troughton followed, and each

Surrey v. Kent

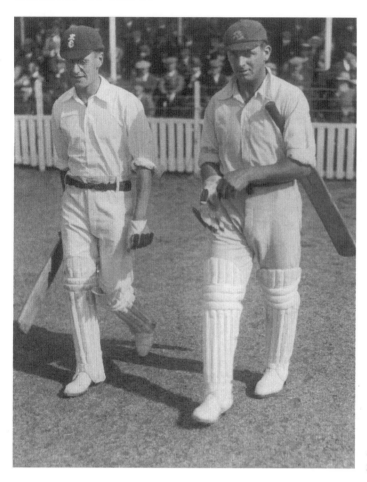

M. Howell and J.W. Hitch
going out to bat.

played so well that the chances of a drawn game increased every minute. After the tea interval, however, Troughton was bowled, a brilliant catch by Peach disposed of Hubble, and the balance swung still further against Kent when Fairsevice was bowled by Hitch. Freeman and Johnstone then kept their ends up for a while until Strudwick made his third catch at the wicket and the innings came to an end for 184.

Surrey were left with forty-two minutes in which to score the 95 runs necessary to win the match. It seemed an almost impossible task, but Crawford and Hobbs at once went for the runs and some really amazing hitting began. The first 50 runs were scored in twenty-one minutes and Hobbs who, at first, was not quite as free as Crawford, took up the running and a race began for the winning hit. This was made by Hobbs exactly thirty-two minutes after the innings had begun. There was a great scene after the match was over, Hobbs being carried shoulder high into the pavilion.

Kent, for their part, played an uphill game in a fine spirit, which showed itself at its best in the last few minutes of the game, when rain fell and the Kent eleven stayed on the field to accept defeat. The crowd of some 12,000 people had the double satisfaction of paying tribute to the world's greatest batsman and of watching him take part with success in one of the most exciting finishes on record.

SURREY *v.* KENT

Played at The Oval on 18th and 19th August 1919 [2-day Match]   Toss: Not known
Surrey won by 10 wickets

KENT

E. Humphreys	c Ducat b Hitch	59	c Knight b Hitch	1
H.T.W. Hardinge	run out	31	c Strudwick b Rushby	25
J. Seymour	b Hitch	0	b Hitch	0
F.E. Woolley	b Crawford	55	c Hobbs b Crawford	29
L.P. Hedges	b Hitch	1	c Strudwick b Rushby	12
*J.C. Hubble	b Rushby	1	c Peach b Lockton	40
G.E.C. Wood	b Rushby	0	lbw b Rushby	5
#L.H.W. Troughton	c Rushby b Crawford	15	b Lockton	41
C.P. Johnstone	b Hitch	21	not out	9
W.J. Fairservice	not out	24	b Hitch	0
A.P. Freeman	run out	0	c Strudwick b Hitch	5
Extras	b 8, lb 3	11	b 13, lb 3, w 1	17
Total	**(all out)**	**218**	**(all out)**	**184**

SURREY

J.B. Hobbs	c & b Fairservice	17	not out	47
*D.J. Knight	c Hubble b Woolley	14		
A. Ducat	b Johnstone	76		
A. Sandham	lbw b Freeman	11		
H.S. Harrison	c Hubble b Woolley	66		
J.N. Crawford	c Hedges b Fairservice	28	[2] not out	48
H.A. Peach	b Freeman	17		
J.W. Hitch	b Fairservice	42		
J.H. Lockton	c Johnstone b Woolley	13		
#H. Strudwick	not out	3		
T. Rushby	b Fairservice	1		
Extras	b 15, lb 5	20	b 1	1
Total	**(all out)**	**308**	**(for no wickets)**	**96**

Bowling

SURREY	O	M	R	W	O	M	R	W
Hitch	20	6	58	4	26.3	4	64	4
Rushby	23.5	7	81	2	24	10	39	3
Crawford	15	3	29	2	16	3	37	1
Lockton	11	2	39	0	13	4	21	2
Peach					3	1	6	0

KENT	O	M	R	W	O	M	R	W
Fairservice	33.2	8	96	4	5	0	26	0
Woolley	46	15	101	3	6	0	54	0
Freeman	23	5	62	2	1.1	0	15	0
Humphreys	7	1	20	0				
Johnstone	3	0	9	1				

FALL OF WICKETS

	K	S	K	S
1st	68	22	3	–
2nd	69	39	3	–
3rd	104	78	42	–
4th	130	156	69	–
5th	131	205	74	–
6th	137	234	80	–
7th	164	284	160	–
8th	182	304	163	–
9th	207	306	168	–
10th	218	308	184	–

Umpires: H.R. Butt and T.M. Russell

SURREY v. MIDDLESEX

Date: 28, 30-31 August 1920

Location: Lord's

County Championship

In 1920 the race for the County Championship was very close. Surrey lost to Middlesex at Lord's in a match reported in *The Times* as a match that will surely never be forgotten by those who were lucky enough to be present. The game had attracted a considerable amount of attention, partly owing to its important bearing on the result, but still more because it was to be 'Plum' Warner's last match in county cricket. From the moment that the first ball was bowled on Saturday there was an atmosphere quite foreign to the usual county match and the last day's cricket was followed with the keenest interest, culminating in scenes of the wildest enthusiasm. It was undoubtedly a great victory for Middlesex, but it was also a fine piece of sportsmanship on the part of the Surrey team who, undaunted by failures, played to win the game outright, rather than be content with a win on the first innings. The glory of the victory was, of course, reflected in the fact that it gave Middlesex the championship, and one could well understand Warner's feelings when, in a short speech from the dressing room, he told the crowd he was the happiest man alive. Surrey finished in third place.

A crowd of 25,000 saw the first day's play. Middlesex won the toss and scored 258 for 8 in a full day. The importance of the occasion seemed a little too much for some of the players, so that among the many failures Warner's success shone all the more brightly. He clearly saved his side from a disaster. Going in to bat after 3 wickets had fallen for 35, he was still undefeated at the close of play, having been at the wicket while 223 precious runs were scored.

On the Monday Surrey started their innings just after midday with Hobbs and Sandham posting 50 runs in as many minutes. Hobbs then fell to Hearne and the remainder of the innings belonged to Andy Sandham, who played a superb innings of 167 not out, enabling Surrey to lead by 73 on the first innings. Sandham's innings was described as being great as appearing to be the most imperturbable of players, he was never too slow to be interesting with a splendid variety of strokes. On the Tuesday Middlesex set out to score as fast as possible, in order to leave Surrey just the right amount of time in which either to get out or win. In the morning session Skeet and Lee added 153 runs, but Lee was bowled by Hitch when only 9 runs had been added in the afternoon after the lunch break. Skeet was then caught in the slips, after both batsmen had played their part admirably. Despite their best efforts the other Middlesex batsmen failed to score fast and wickets fell regularly. The innings was declared closed at 3.40 p.m., setting Surrey the task of scoring 244 in three hours. Hobbs was caught in the slips at 22 and Howell joined Sandham and attacked the bowling. With the score rising, Stevens replaced Haig at the Nursery end and had Howell stumped. Sandham and Shepherd kept the score up with the clock but Stevens broke the partnership by having Shepherd beautifully caught in the deep off a straight high drive. Wickets then fell regularly and Middlesex ran out winners at 6.10 p.m.

Andy Sandham batting against Hampshire in 1937.

SURREY v. MIDDLESEX

Played at Lord's on 28th, 30th and 31st August 1920 [3-day Match]   Toss: Middlesex
Middlesex won by 55 runs

MIDDLESEX

C.H.L. Skeet	c Ducat b Rushby	2	c Fender b Hitch		106
H.W. Lee	c Hitch b Fender	12	b Hitch		108
J.W. Hearne	c & b Hitch	15	lbw b Rushby		26
E.H. Hendren	b Reay	41	c Sandham b Rushby		5
*P.F. Warner	b Rushby	79	(9) not out		14
F.T. Mann	c & b Fender	12	(5) c Peach b Fender		22
N.E. Haig	b Reay	18	(6) b Rushby		1
G.T.S. Stevens	b Fender	53	(7) not out		21
H.K. Longman	b Fender	0			
#H.R. Murrell	c Ducat b Hitch	9	(8) b Reay		0
F.J. Durston	not out	0			
Extras	b 12, lb 12, nb 3	27	b 8, lb 4, w 1		13
Total	**(all out)**	**268**	**(for 7 wickets declared)**		**316**

SURREY

J.B. Hobbs	c Mann b Hearne	24	c Lee b Haig		10
A. Sandham	not out	167	c & b Hearne		68
M. Howell	c Murrell b Durston	7	st Murrell b Stevens		25
T.F. Shepherd	c Murrell b Durston	0	c Hendren b Stevens		26
H.A. Peach	hit wkt b Stevens	18	(6) b Stevens		11
A. Ducat	st Murrell b Lee	49	(7) lbw b Hearne		7
*P.G.H. Fender	c Haig b Durston	30	(5) b Durston		1
J.W. Hitch	b Durston	1	(8) b Stevens		6
G.M. Reay	c Haig b Lee	6	b Hearne		5
#H. Strudwick	b Hearne	9	b Stevens		10
T. Rushby	not out	6	not out		7
Extras	b 17, lb 5, nb 2	24	b 11, lb 1		12
Total	**(for 9 wickets declared)**	**341**	**(all out)**		**188**

Bowling

SURREY	O	M	R	W	O	M	R	W
Hitch	32.1	10	66	2	20	5	71	2
Rushby	23	9	48	2	22	7	73	3
Fender	28	4	76	4	16.5	2	70	1
Reay	26	17	31	2	18	1	61	1
Ducat	3	1	10	0	3	0	12	0
Shepherd	6	3	10	0	4	0	16	0

MIDDLESEX	O	M	R	W	O	M	R	W
Durston	30	9	97	4	14	1	42	1
Haig	10	4	25	0	8	0	19	1
Stevens	16	0	72	1	13.4	0	61	5
Hearne	24	8	57	2	11	0	37	3
Lee	15	2	66	2	4	0	17	0

FALL OF WICKETS

	M	S	M	S
1st	4	59	208	22
2nd	23	78	249	62
3rd	35	82	254	120
4th	88	128	261	122
5th	109	227	265	143
6th	149	275	290	155
7th	239	277	291	166
8th	245	312	–	169
9th	264	335	–	176
10th	268	–	–	188

Umpires: J. Blake and G.P. Harrison.

SURREY v. SOMERSET

Date: 15, 17-18 August 1925   **County Championship**
Location: Taunton

In July 1925, Jack Hobbs scored a century against Kent and became the first batsman to reach 2,000 runs for the season. He now stood one century short of the record of W.G. Grace for the most centuries ever scored in first-class cricket. Crowds, cameras and newsmen flocked after him wherever he went. 'Will he make a century today?' was the constant question. Match after match went by until he arrived at Taunton in mid-August. Yet again a huge crowd arrived to see if Hobbs could equal Grace's record.

On the Saturday, Somerset batted first and were bowled out for 167 by 4 p.m. With a tea interval at 5 p.m., Surrey had two-and-a-quarter hours' batting on the first evening. At 6 p.m., with forty-five minutes left, Hobbs had made 53. Suddenly he accelerated and doubled his rate of scoring. The crowd grew more and more excited, but Hobbs just lost his race against the clock and finished on 91 not out. He had had one piece of fortune. With his score on 86 he called his partner, D.J. Knight, for a risky run. Hobbs was almost down the pitch before Knight could start. It seemed certain that Hobbs would be run out but Knight deliberately crossed him, thus throwing away his own wicket in order that Hobbs might go on batting. It was a fine piece of self-sacrifice.

Six thousand people, a vast crowd for Taunton in 1925, were present on the Monday. At 11 a.m. the queue at the gate was nearly half-a-mile long. Hobbs played with the greatest care. In obtaining the necessary 9 runs Hobbs had 17 balls bowled to him. A single brought up his century and the cheers, it was said, could be heard at Taunton station. Crowds gathered outside the Hobbs' shop in Fleet Street and clapped and cheered. Fender came onto the field with a champagne glass, although whether it contained champagne or ginger ale for Hobbs, the teetotaller, none would say. Congratulations poured upon the very popular man and batsman. The news of Hobbs' performance dominated all the newspapers, but few were prepared for what was to come, so intent had they been to capture the moment when Hobbs equalled Grace's record.

Jack Hobbs. *(Empics)*

After the tension of Hobbs' hundred, the dismissal of Jardine, who might have been caught in the slips twice in one over from Robertson-Glasgow, came as a slight relief. Jardine was run out going for a fourth run and Fender made several glorious strokes during his stay of fifty minutes, his straight and off-driving being magnificent. He was mainly responsible for the third hundred being scored in forty minutes. The Surrey innings ended soon after the lunch interval. The best cricket of the day and the match came in the afternoon when MacBryan and Young opened the Somerset second innings with a stand of 184 and the score at the end of the second day was 256 for 3 wickets.

The completion of the Somerset innings on Tuesday morning saw Johnson mistime a well-disguised slower ball from Fender by placing it rather than hitting it straight to mid-off. White made a number of good strokes before providing Strudwick with the second of three good catches. At 2.15 p.m. Hobbs and Sandham went out to open the Surrey second innings with 183 needed to

Jack Hobbs in full flight.

win. There were only a few hundred people present. Surrey's second innings was full of interest. The point was whether Sandham would score slowly enough to allow Hobbs to break the record and at the same time not jeopardize his side's chances of winning. After an hour's play the score was 73 with Hobbs on 38 and Sandham 30. Inspection of the pitch during the luncheon interval revealed the fact that it had slightly crumbled, but this was chiefly in the place that would have suited a leg-break bowler of the type that was not playing. The fact that the first 3 overs bowled by White to Hobbs were all maidens, therefore, was not entirely due to the batsmen's desire to go slowly.

The state of the pitch compelled extra care be taken, as was clearly seen when Young, going on at 57, was able to make the ball turn sharply from the off. Young began with a maiden over to Hobbs who, in Young's next 5 overs covered up and ignored the ball altogether more often than he had done during the whole of his first innings. Sandham took twenty-five minutes to make his next 6 runs, while Hobbs made 22 in the same time, reaching his fifty with a fine hit through the covers after having been in for sixty-five minutes. With the total at 95 Sandham was nearly run out, Bridges failing to gather an indifferent return. Sandham reached his fifty at 4 p.m. with three brilliant strokes on the on-side, all off Robertson-Glasgow.

SURREY v. SOMERSET

Andy Sandham.

At this stage Hobbs had to make 25 of the 47 needed to win with the tea interval looming, and White bowling a very accurate length. Longrigg was tried with a negative kind of slow bowling from the Pavilion end. Hobbs had a good look at the first 4 balls and then took 8 off the next 2. In the same bowler's next over another unintentional full toss found its proper destination, bringing Hobbs' score to 95, with 25 still wanted to win. With Hobbs' score on 96 White changed his bowling, making it quite clear that not a single run was to be presented to the batsmen. A run later Hobbs missed a swerving full toss from Young, nearly giving a stumping chance. Sandham then played a maiden over with the care suitable for the occasion. In Young's next over the old familiar push past short leg secured the required single and thus at 4.38 p.m. was Grace's record of centuries broken and a new record for a total of centuries in a season – fourteen – was created. Sandham finished off the 10-wicket victory at 4.44 p.m. Hobbs hit fourteen fours and gave no semblance of a chance and the innings as a whole was much more characteristic of him than the previous one had been. Sandham's share in Hobbs' achievement must not be overlooked. Indeed, he played a very big part in it.

At the close of play there was a lot of cheering before the pavilion and Hobbs had to make a speech in which he expressed himself as the happiest man on earth, regretting only he had not accomplished this performance at The Oval.

Hobbs continued to play for Surrey until 1934, scoring centuries at regular intervals and to this day holds the all-time record of 197 centuries in first-class cricket. On his retirement he was present at the ceremony to open the Hobbs Gates at The Oval. He was a respected member of the community and the first professional cricketer to be knighted for his contribution to the game. Affectionally known as 'The Master', his birthday, 16 December, is celebrated to this day with a luncheon being held at The Oval by members of 'The Masters Club'.

SURREY v. SOMERSET

Played at Taunton on 15th, 17th and 18th August 1925 [3-day Match]   Toss: Somerset
Surrey won by 10 wickets

SOMERSET

J.C.W. MacBryan	b Holmes	6	b Fender		109
A. Young	c Sadler b Lockton	58	c Strudwick b Sadler		71
T.E.S. Francis	b Sadler	0	(7) c Strudwick b Sadler		12
*J.C. White	b Sadler	1	c Strudwick b Sadler		30
P.R. Johnson	c & b Lockton	30	c Peach b Fender		16
E.F. Longrigg	b Sadler	5	run out		4
R.A. Ingle	b Fender	22	(3) c Shepherd b Peach		23
G.E. Hunt	b Lockton	4	b Fender		59
R.C. Robertson-Glasgow	c Jardine b Lockton	4	c Sadler b Fender		5
J.J. Bridges	c & b Shepherd	25	b Fender		26
#M.L. Hill	not out	0	not out		1
Extras	lb 8, w 4	12	b 9, lb 5, nb 4		18
Total	**(all out)**	**167**	**(all out)**		**374**

SURREY

J.B. Hobbs	c Hill b Bridges	101	not out		101
A. Sandham	c Longrigg b Bridges	13	not out		74
D.J. Knight	run out	34			
T.F. Shepherd	b White	0			
D.R. Jardine	run out	47			
E.R.T. Holmes	c Hill b Robertson-Glasgow	24			
*P.G.H. Fender	st Hill b Young	59			
H.A. Peach	b Young	20			
W.C.H. Sadler	c Johnson b Young	25			
#H. Strudwick	not out	10			
J.H. Lockton	absent hurt				
Extras	b15, lb 8, nb 3	26	b6, lb 1, nb 1		8
Total	**(all out)**	**359**	**(for no wicket)**		**183**

Bowling

SURREY	O	M	R	W	O	M	R	W
Sadler	16	4	28	3	21	5	59	2
Holmes	6	2	12	1	17	0	56	0
Fender	13	3	39	1	35.5	8	120	5
Lockton	16	4	36	4	9	2	15	1
Peach	9	2	21	0	20	7	46	1
Shepherd	6.3	1	19	1	21	5	60	0

SOMERSET	O	M	R	W	O	M	R	W
Robertson-Glasgow	26	1	144	1	6	0	42	0
Bridges	37	5	115	2	11	3	27	0
White	29	13	51	1	14	6	34	0
Hunt	4	1	14	0	8	4	15	0
Young	5.3	1	9	3	15.5	1	39	0
Longrigg					3	0	18	0

FALL OF WICKETS

	So	Su	So	Su
1st	11	50	184	–
2nd	12	146	203	–
3rd	16	148	228	–
4th	93	170	262	–
5th	110	221	268	–
6th	112	260	268	–
7th	118	322	310	–
8th	126	325	352	–
9th	163	359	373	–
10th	167		374	–

Umpires: H. Draper and H.I. Young

SURREY v. NOTTINGHAMSHIRE

Date: 26, 28-29 May 1928   **County Championship**
Location: Trent Bridge

This Whitsun match attracted 10,000 people on the first day. The story of the Nottinghamshire innings in the first two sessions revolved around Gunn and the changing phases of his innings. Whysall was out early but Gunn and Walker took the score to 108 by lunch. Gunn reached his fifty after the interval 1 ball in front of Walker. Gunn had made batting look ridiculously easy but, when in the nineties, he lapsed into passiveness and it was not until 3.30 p.m. that he reached his hundred. Meanwhile, the other Nottinghamshire batsmen were not doing too well and wickets fell regularly during the afternoon. Gunn was bowled soon after tea trying to cut Shepherd and then Barratt and Staples altered the whole complexion of the game in an hour by adding 167 runs in eighty-five minutes. Barratt proceeded to show how very fast a big man could score off tiring bowling by taking chances. Three times he drove the ball for six and Staples, although rather less spectacular, kept pace with him. After each of them had reached 50 Barratt went rapidly ahead and when caught in the slips he had made 96 in eighty-five minutes. He had just missed what would have been his first century but he and Staples had appeared to make Nottinghamshire safe from defeat.

The Bank Holiday Monday found 20,000 in the ground and the last two Nottinghamshire wickets added 49, with Staples also just failing to score a hundred. In the remainder of the morning session Surrey scored 68 for the loss of Sandham. Hobbs quickly showed that he did not intend to take any risks against Larwood but did survive when Whysall at first slip let a ball go through his hands to the boundary. After lunch Larwood bowled 5 overs magnificent enough to make the slightest breath of criticism ungenerous. Ducat continually played the kind of indeterminate strokes a fast bowler thrives on and Hobbs played at some balls in a way that must have made Whysall feel he would be given a chance of atoning for his mistake, but Hobbs went grimly on with the task of making runs. Every now and then he made a stroke that reminded the crowd that it was indeed him batting and they must have been sorry when he was caught with the score at 199. Wickets fell quickly as Larwood picked up 3 deserved wickets and Surrey were all out for 288, but the follow-on was not enforced.

Nottinghamshire must have regretted this decision as Gunn was out with only 5 runs scored and 3 more wickets fell for another 10 runs by the close. Their captain, A.W. Carr, could not have foreseen his team's utter collapse but the fact remained that their only chance of winning would have been to put Surrey in

Alan Peach.

again on the previous evening. Fender and Peach did their best to be as terrible as the batsmen were prepared to think they were and, with nobody to test them, that was perfectly sufficient. Payton was out to the second ball of the morning, making the score 15 for 5. The story of the rest of the innings was one of bad batting opposed to bowling conscious of its moral advantage, and resolute enough to drive it home.

With Surrey needing 220 to win Surrey lost Hobbs and Ducat for 3 runs. Larwood took the first over and Hobbs was out to his second ball, caught at second slip. Ducat lost his middle stump to Samuel Staples and had Larwood taken the further wicket his bowling deserved anything might have happened. As it turned out Sandham and Shepherd took the score to 145 before Shepherd was stumped. The life soon went out of the bowling and there was never much doubt that Surrey would go on to win the match.

SURREY *v.* NOTTINGHAMSHIRE

Played at Trent Bridge on 26th, 28th and 29th May 1928 [3-day Match]   Toss: Not known
Surrey won by 7 wickets

NOTTINGHAMSHIRE

G. Gunn	b Shepherd	122	c Brooks b Peach		4
W.W. Whysall	c & b Peach	10	c & b Fender		4
W. Walker	c Brooks b Fenley	51	c Jardine b Fender		5
*A.W. Carr	b Shepherd	1	[5] c Brooks b Fender		22
W.R.D. Payton	b Fender	4	[6] c Ducat b Peach		0
#B. Lilley	b Fender	12	[7] b Fender		2
H. Larwood	b Peach	20	[8] b Peach		0
A. Staples	c Jardine b Fender	94	[9] c Jardine b Peach		0
F. Barratt	c Fender b Peach	96	[10] not out		0
S.J. Staples	c Sandham b Fender	28	[11] c Jardine b Peach		7
T.L. Richmond	not out	6	[4] b Peach		1
Extras	b 10, lb 1, w 2	13	b 4, lb 1		5
Total	**(all out)**	**457**	**(all out)**		**50**

SURREY

J.B. Hobbs	c Whysall b A. Staples	114	c S.J. Staples b Larwood		0
A. Sandham	b S.J. Staples	9	not out		92
A. Ducat	lbw b Richmond	45	b S.J. Staples		2
T.F. Shepherd	c S.J. Staples b Larwood	26	st Lilley b Richmond		68
D.R. Jardine	lbw b Richmond	22	not out		36
T.H. Barling	b S.J. Staples	10			
R.J. Gregory	lbw b Barratt	13			
*P.G.H. Fender	c S.J. Staples b Larwood	3			
H.A. Peach	c & b S.J. Staples	25			
S. Fenley	b Larwood	5			
#E.W.J. Brooks	not out	0			
Extras	b 9, lb 4, nb 2, w 1	16	b14, lb 8		22
Total	**(all out)**	**288**	**(for 3 wickets)**		**220**

Bowling

SURREY	O	M	R	W	O	M	R	W
Fender	38	11	92	4	13	4	21	4
Peach	44	7	143	3	12.2	6	24	6
Fenley	28	2	83	1				
Shepherd	32	8	63	2				
Gregory	16	2	61	0				
Jardine	1	0	2	0				

NOTTINGHAMSHIRE	O	M	R	W	O	M	R	W
Larwood	25.1	7	47	3	13	2	35	1
Barratt	18	4	37	1	8	3	15	0
S.J. Staples	23	5	56	3	20	3	63	1
A. Staples	14	1	43	1	10.1	1	30	0
Richmond	23	4	89	2	17	1	50	1
Gunn					1	0	5	0

FALL OF WICKETS

	N	S	N	S
1st	13	32	5	0
2nd	121	136	14	3
3rd	124	190	15	145
4th	160	211	15	–
5th	188	232	15	–
6th	228	253	32	–
7th	238	270	39	–
8th	405	270	43	–
9th	436	288	43	–
10th	457	288	50	–

Umpires: J.H. King and W. Phillips

SURREY v. KENT

Date: 28, 30-31 July 1928   **County Championship**
Location: The Oval

With a man like Percy Fender as captain, it was always unwise to write off Surrey. What he achieved with a limited bowling attack on the placid Oval wickets almost qualified him for membership of the Magic Circle. In his time as captain Surrey always had the batting, but the bowling was threadbare; yet somehow Fender would conjure up victories by a mixture of cheek, cunning, tactical sagacity and luck. Kent came to The Oval at the top of the table. Lancashire, lying second, had just beaten them by 8 wickets, but neutrals wanted Kent to lift the title.

Fender won the toss and he would have fielded had he the bowlers to capitalise on a wicket that favoured spin. He rightly reasoned that it was up to his batsmen to get a good enough score to enable them to attack Kent in the last innings when presumably the ball would be turning even more. Within a quarter of an hour, 'Tich' Freeman, the Kent spinner who had just completed 200 wickets for the season, was on at the Pavilion End. Hobbs and Ducat were both out to catches at slip from sharply turning leg-breaks and at lunch Surrey were in trouble at 81 for 5. Fender, as usual, opted for a positive response and tried to hit the spinners out of the attack, but he soon cut a long-hop to deep point and retired, cursing himself. Marriott wrapped up the innings with 3 wickets in 9 balls and already it seemed as if Kent were impregnable.

. At the end of the first day Kent's lead was already 29 with 6 wickets in hand following aggressive batting by Woolley and support from Ames and Legge. The next day Legge went on to make 111 but then Ames was unluckily run out and Kent rather lost their way, ending up with a lead of 152 when they might have fancied at least 300.

When Hobbs and Sandham started off like a train Kent had their spinners on within half an hour. Hobbs made a beautiful hundred and, characteristically, gave away his wicket after he had passed three figures. No one else in the Surrey side matched Hobbs' mastery that day. When Gregory went first ball, Surrey were 215 for 7, a lead of just 63, with Fender and Peach the last remaining hopes. Fender played the watchful role, while Peach hit well with an engagingly crooked bat. They managed to set Kent a target that was far from derisory, although 131 on a blameless pitch was comfortably within their compass.

Percy Fender – one of the great Surrey captains.

After heavy overnight rain there was no play on the third day until 12.30 p.m. Fender, ever alert to the psychological nuances, brought all the Surrey side out to look at the wicket and indulged in agonised thumb-pressing, all to no avail as Kent were 58 without loss at lunch. At 64, Fender got Ashdown, Woolley was dismissed for 14 and Hardinge for 25. Now the self-belief began to flood through the Surrey ranks. Peach bowled an immaculate length, Fender went through his bewildering variations in spin and the fielding was keenness itself. Ames, Legge and Deed went cheaply and it was now 103 for 6. At 105, Valentine was easily run out going for a second run to a misfield by Sandham. Longfield tried to hit his way out of the mess, unsuccessfully, Gover caught Freeman and Marriott was caught for a duck. Kent contrived to lose the game, with their last 6 wickets falling for 13 runs, but it was Fender who first made them conceive of defeat. With subtle gamesmanship, the occasional histrionic gesture and some shrewd field placing, he let Kent think a target of 131 was difficult.

SURREY v. KENT

Played at The Oval on 28th, 30th and 31st July 1928 [3-day Match]   Toss: Surrey
Surrey won by 14 runs

SURREY

J.B. Hobbs	c Legge b Freeman	6	c Beslee b Freeman	109
A. Sandham	c Freeman b Marriott	29	lbw b Freeman	17
A. Ducat	c Woolley b Freeman	22	c Marriott b Freeman	33
T.F. Shepherd	c Marriott b Woolley	6	lbw b Marriott	17
T.H. Barling	b Freeman	6	lbw b Freeman	17
H.M. Garland-Wells	c Freeman b Marriott	5	lbw b Marriott	2
*P.G.H. Fender	c Beslee b Freeman	22	c Legge b Beslee	42
R.J. Gregory	lbw b Marriott	3	b Freeman	0
H.A. Peach	not out	6	c Ashdown b Marriott	25
#E.W.J. Brooks	st Ames b Marriott	2	not out	1
A.R. Gover	c Ames b Marriott	0	c Ames b Beslee	0
Extras	b 6, lb 3, nb 2	11	b11, lb 7, nb 1	19
Total	**(all out)**	**131**	**(all out)**	**282**

KENT

H.T.H. Hardinge	c Fender b Garland-Wells	38	c Gregory b Fender	25
W.H. Ashdown	c Gregory b Gover	9	b Fender	44
F.E. Woolley	c Garland-Wells b Shepherd	51	c Shepherd b Fender	14
#L.E.G. Ames	run out	96	c Barling b Peach	8
J.A. Deed	b Fender	10	c Brooks b Peach	5
*G.B. Legge	c Fender b Garland-Wells	52	c Brooks b Fender	6
T.C. Longfield	c Fender b Garland-Wells	2	not out	6
B.H. Valentine	b Fender	2	run out	1
G.P. Beslee	b Garland-Wells	0	c Fender b Peach	6
A.P. Freeman	not out	4	c Gover b Peach	0
C.S. Marriott	c Hobbs b Fender	8	c Garland-Wells b Fender	0
Extras	b 8, lb 1, nb 2	11	b 1	1
Total	**(all out)**	**283**	**(all out)**	**116**

Bowling

KENT	O	M	R	W	O	M	R	W
Beslee	4	1	7	0	9	3	26	2
Ashdown	4	4	0	0	11	2	35	0
Marriott	24.5	12	41	5	29	3	81	3
Freeman	28	8	58	4	31	4	101	5
Woolley	5	1	14	1				
Longfield					3	0	9	0
Hardinge					2	0	11	0

SURREY	O	M	R	W	O	M	R	W
Gover	24	4	76	1				
Peach	9	0	34	0	23	6	36	4
Garland-Wells	18	7	35	4	7	1	25	0
Fender	26.4	9	78	3	23	8	53	5
Gregory	6	1	19	0				
Shepherd	17	2	30	1	2	1	1	0

FALL OF WICKETS

	S	K	S	K
1st	9	13	44	64
2nd	53	86	111	80
3rd	61	111	173	89
4th	69	142	191	92
5th	77	253	193	103
6th	103	260	215	103
7th	123	262	215	105
8th	123	263	254	116
9th	131	264	282	116
10th	131	283	282	116

Umpires: J. Moss and W.A. Buswell

Surrey v. Middlesex

Date: 6, 8-9 August 1932

Location: The Oval

County Championship

Middlesex started badly by losing Sims with only 19 runs on the board, but Lee and Hearne made batting look easy enough. Lee was scoring much the faster of the two until at 63 he mishit a short ball to be caught at mid-on. Hendren hit a full pitch carelessly to leg for Brown to make a good catch high at square leg. Killick and Hearne progressed but found it difficult to get the ball away. After lunch Parker came on and bowled straight enough to take 4 wickets for 15 runs in 10 overs and 5 balls, but the truth was that many batsmen threw their wickets away wantonly and Middlesex slumped to be all out for 141.

Ratcliffe opened with Hobbs but fell caught at the wicket with the score at 27 and, 2 runs later, Shepherd was caught off the shoulder of his bat. Fender, promoted to go in second wicket down, made a few good strokes but was bowled by Hulme at 59. This was the extent of the bowlers' success until the last over of the day. Hobbs and Jardine batted as if they had seconds to spare in which to place the ball wherever they chose. But just when the crowd were preparing to applaud another century by Hobbs, their hero banged a ball into mid-off's hands and stumps were pulled up for the day.

The second day saw Surrey take their score from 184 for 4 to 540 before the innings was declared closed at 3.30 p.m., so scoring 356 runs in 195 minutes. Freddie Brown scored 212, which included seven sixes and fifteen fours in three hours, and his partnership with Maurice Allom produced 155 runs in a minute or two over the hour. The true pleasure of it all was that at no time did the batting cease to be batting; there was no wild slogging to bowling that maintained a commendable accuracy and fielding that remained to the end splendidly keen.

Middlesex had to go in again 399 runs behind and at the close of play had made 134 runs for the loss of 1 wicket. Jardine began the bowling on the last day with Allom and Parker, but no wicket fell until

Freddie Brown.

they were replaced by Brown and Fender. The score by lunch had risen to 241 for 2 with Sims completing his first century in a county match. Only 7 runs had been added before Sims was bowled by a good ball from Parker that came back sharply. Killick fell at 268 and Surrey missed a great chance when Hendren, who had then scored 84, was missed at mid-off from a short ball from Fender. The eighth wicket fell with Middlesex still 61 runs behind with two hours to play, but Price, who stayed for one-and-a-half hours, helped Hendren to clear off the runs and establish a lead of 44. Hendren was brilliantly run out and Durston batted for twenty minutes and when he was out it left Surrey the task of scoring 57 runs in twenty minutes.

The winning hit was made off the last ball of the match after a period of the wildest excitement, with batsmen running backwards and forwards from the pavilion to the wicket, catches galore being missed, and fieldsmen performing terrific feats of agility to punish the short run. It was left to Douglas Jardine, at the last possible moment, to drive the ball hard against the pavilion railings for the winning hit.

SURREY *v.* MIDDLESEX

Played at The Oval on 6th, 8th, and 9th August 1932 [3-day Match]   Toss: Middlesex
Surrey won by 6 wickets

MIDDLESEX

H.W. Lee	c Parker b Fender	40	c Jardine b Fender		25
J.M. Sims	lbw b Allom	6	b Parker		103
J.W. Hearne	c Brooks b Parker	57	c Fender b Brown		61
E.H. Hendren	c Brown b Owen	4	run out		145
E.T. Killick	b Brown	11	lbw b Brown		10
J.H.A. Hulme	b Brown	0	b Brown		24
H.J. Enthoven	b Parker	13	b Brown		8
*N.E. Haig	c Ratcliffe b Parker	2	[9] c Allom b Brown		0
G.E. Hart	b Parker	0	[8] c Block b Fender		1
#W.F.F. Price	b Brown	0	not out		35
F.J. Durston	not out	0	c Parker b Fender		10
Extras	b 4, lb 2, w 2	8	b 19, lb 8, nb 1, w 5		33
Total	**(all out)**	**141**	**(all out)**		**455**

SURREY

J.B. Hobbs	c Enthoven b Lee	92			
A. Ratcliffe	c Price b Durston	12	[5] not out		1
T.F. Shepherd	c Hearne b Durston	1	[1] run out		22
P.G.H. Fender	b Hulme	12	[3] c Lee b Haig		0
*D.R. Jardine	c Durston b Lee	126	[6] not out		10
S.A. Block	b Durston	3	[4] run out		19
F.R. Brown	c Killick b Haig	212	[2] c Lee b Durston		4
J.F. Parker	st Price b Sims	8			
#E.W.J. Brooks	lbw b Sims	3			
M.J.C. Allom	not out	57			
J.G. Owen					
Extras	b 1, lb 9, nb 1, w 3	14	w 1		1
Total	**(for 9 wickets declared)**	**540**	**(for 4 wickets)**		**57**

Bowling

SURREY	O	M	R	W	O	M	R	W
Allom	12	2	23	1	42	6	82	0
Parker	20	7	36	4	40	6	104	1
Brown	20.5	7	38	3	48	14	81	5
Fender	6	0	26	1	40	8	123	3
Owen	8	4	10	1	9	4	19	0
Jardine					3	1	13	0

MIDDLESEX	O	M	R	W	O	M	R	W
Durston	42	6	122	3	4	0	32	1
Hulme	23	2	93	1	3	0	24	1
Lee	30	5	115	2				
Sims	12	1	54	2				
Hearne	20	3	86	0				
Haig	8.4	0	56	1				

FALL OF WICKETS

	M	S	M	S
1st	19	27	44	8
2nd	63	29	157	9
3rd	78	59	248	45
4th	103	184	268	46
5th	103	191	318	–
6th	136	338	331	–
7th	138	377	338	–
8th	140	385	338	–
9th	141	540	443	–
10th	141	–	455	–

Umpires: W. Bestwick and C.N. Woolley

SURREY v. MIDDLESEX

Date: 8-10 August 1934   County Championship

Location: The Oval

Before lunch on the first day Middlesex, who won the toss, lost 5 wickets for 88 runs, and in every case the bowler thoroughly deserved his wicket. Watts took the first wicket, Hart fell to Fender and Hearne to Garland-Wells. A stand between Hulme and Hendren, which looked likely to retrieve the situation, was broken when Hendren was bowled by Fender. After lunch the collapse continued. Surrey should have finished off the innings quickly but failed to do so. Hulme advanced to reach his fifty and was supported by Haig, the innings finally closing at 184. Surrey got away to a bad start by losing both Sandham and Squires with only 16 runs on the board. Winlaw and Gregory then settled into a lengthy stand, taking few risks, to leave the County on 121 for 2 at the close of play.

On the second day Gregory, who scored 121, reached 2,000 runs in a season for the first time in his career. Surrey continued to quietly consolidate their advantage but the main interest was in the bowling of Cedric Smith, who kept a length over a long spell. Winlaw was first to fall to a catch in the gully and 4 runs later Barling was out to the same fielder. Errol Holmes came in to play an innings in which there were bad strokes as well as good. Gregory was out at 265 when he drove a ball from Hearne hard back and the bowler took the catch low down with his right hand. At lunch Surrey were 89 runs ahead with 4 wickets in hand. Afterwards, Garland-Wells proceeded to deal almost exclusively in fours, making 43 in thirty-five minutes and Watts meanwhile journeyed adventurously into the forties.

Middlesex began their second innings, some 175 runs behind, and Price and Hart did nobly for their side by scoring 50 runs together in under forty minutes, which saw Gover taken off. The light was far from good and at tea Middlesex were 61 for no wicket. With the score at 90 Hart was brilliantly caught and bowled by Fender, at 101 Hearne was bowled and at 114 Fender hit Hendrix's off stump.

On the last day the Surrey out-cricket was, apart from some isolated overs by Fender, Watts and Gover, deplorable and Middlesex were allowed to carry their score to 292. Surrey, set 118 runs to win, lost Gregory before lunch. Afterwards Allen, bowling from the Pavilion end with the wind at his back, and Smith made a Middlesex victory a probability rather than a phantom hope. Winlaw, in trying to hook, played the first ball he received on to his face and retired, badly hurt, heroically to resume his innings later. Allen took the wickets of Holmes and Watts in one over. Sandham, in trying to hook Smith, was caught at square leg and Barling was out to a catch at second slip playing a distinctly feeble shot. Garland-Wells decided to hit out and raised the total to 96 in company with Fender, and then a tiring Allen hit Fender's off stump. Garland-Wells fell 6 runs later followed by Gover playing an agricultural stroke to leave the last pair to score 14 runs. Winlaw, pale, stitches over one eye, joined Brooks and then played a curious stroke to a slowish ball from Smith, was hit on the back of the head and collapsed. He then got up and hit the next ball for four to win this exciting match.

Bob Gregory being caught in a match against Somerset in 1937.

SURREY v. MIDDLESEX

Played at The Oval on 8th, 9th and 10th August 1934 [3-day Match]   Toss: Middlesex
Surrey won by 1 wicket

MIDDLESEX

G.E. Hart	c Gover b Fender	18	c & b Fender		30
#W.F.F. Price	b Watts	5	c Watts b Holmes		87
J.W. Hearne	c Watts b Garland-Wells	13	b Gover		4
E.H. Hendren	b Fender	15	b Fender		11
J.H.A. Hulme	c Watts b Fender	62	b Watts		49
G.O.B. Allen	c Brooks b Gover	13	lbw b Fender		11
J.L. Guise	c Brooks b Gover	5	c Brooks b Gover		4
J.M. Sims	b Fender	8	b Watts		7
*N.E. Haig	b Holmes	25	b Fender		23
B.L. Muncer	c Holmes b Fender	8	not out		9
C.I.J. Smith	not out	4	c Gregory b Fender		45
Extras	lb 2, w 1, nb 5	8	b 6, lb 6		12
Total	**(all out)**	**184**	**(all out)**		**292**

SURREY

A. Sandham	c Hearne b Smith	5	c Allen b Smith		12
R.J. Gregory	c & b Hearne	121	b Allen		6
H.S. Squires	c Price b Smith	3	c Price b Smith		1
R.D.K. Winlaw	c Sims b Smith	69	not out		4
H.T. Barling	c Sims b Smith	4	(7) c Guise b Smith		2
*E.R.T. Holmes	c Smith b Hulme	37	(5) b Allen		9
E.A. Watts	run out	48	(6) c Hendren b Allen		2
H.M. Garland-Wells	c Hulme b Hearne	43	c Sims b Smith		45
P.G.H. Fender	b Smith	9	b Allen		9
A.R. Gover	lbw b Smith	5	b Smith		1
#E.W.J. Brooks	not out	3	not out		9
Extras	b 6, lb 5, nb 1	12	b 9, lb 8, nb 1		18
Total	**(all out)**	**359**	**(for 9 wickets)**		**118**

Bowling

SURREY	O	M	R	W	O	M	R	W
Gover	16	4	34	2	28	5	101	2
Watts	9	2	34	1	15	3	58	2
Fender	21.4	4	84	5	23.3	2	94	5
Holmes	4	0	12	1	9	1	27	1
Garland-Wells	7	1	12	1				

MIDDLESEX	O	M	R	W	O	M	R	W
Allen	24	6	85	0	16	2	42	4
Smith	42.3	6	98	6	15.3	3	58	5
Sims	20	2	63	0				
Hulme	8	2	20	1				
Hearne	19	0	81	2				

FALL OF WICKETS

	M	S	M	S
1st	18	7	90	15
2nd	39	16	101	20
3rd	45	155	114	33
4th	65	163	140	35
5th	88	222	182	35
6th	96	265	201	43
7th	109	329	207	96
8th	165	349	219	102
9th	180	355	242	104
10th	184	359	292	—

Umpires: A. Dolphin and W. Reeves

SURREY v. NOTTINGHAMSHIRE

Date: 24, 26-27 May 1947   County Championship
Location: Trent Bridge

For many years Surrey played Nottinghamshire over Bank Holiday weekends at Trent Bridge during Whitsun and at The Oval in August. In 1947 there was a crowd of about 7,000 at Trent Bridge on the Saturday to see Nottinghamshire win the toss, bat and try to tame the Surrey opening attack of Alec Bedser and Alf Gover. There was pre-lunch crawl by Walter Keeton, Charlie Harris and Reg Simpson, the first wicket falling at 64 after 100 minutes. Excellent captaincy by Errol Holmes and outstanding out-fielding by Stan Squires kept the scoring rate down, although Nottinghamshire eventually recorded their highest total of the season to date. Keeton batted very slowly, which was completely foreign to his usual methods, scoring 59 out of 131 in nearly three hours. He and Simpson both fell to Alec Bedser when he took a new ball, Keeton being bowled by a perfect length ball that took out his off stump. There were more runs from the other batsmen down the order to produce a fine total and re-establish confidence in batsmen who had previously lacked it.

The Monday attracted a crowd of 15,000, the best attendance since resumption of cricket after the Second World War. David Fletcher had recently joined the Surrey staff and had come into the side to replace Fishlock, who was having an operation for appendicitis, and in his first game had scored 65 and 46 against Somerset. In this match he completed his first century for the county and with Gregory, the oldest man in the side, added 155 in two hours twenty minutes. With Gregory's dismissal, Holmes changed the batting order and sent in Stan Squires and the third wicket advanced the score to 459 in good time. During the evening session, Nottinghamshire wilted under a positive deluge, 34 runs being scored in the first thirty minutes, 68 in the next half-hour, 63 in the third period and 60 in the last thirty minutes to leave Surrey on 443 for 2 wickets at the close.

The third day, before a crowd of 3,000, saw Nottinghamshire away to a bad start. They were relying on their fast bowling duo of Harold Butler and Arthur Jepson, but the later had pulled a muscle in his side. Their fieldsmen then dropped three catches within 7 balls, Squires being put down twice by Harris in the gully, first off Butler then off Stocks, and Fletcher dropped by Voce off Butler. When Squires and Fletcher were finally dismissed there was no relief for the home side as Jack Parker (one six and twelve fours) and Errol Holmes (two sixes and twelve fours) plundered a further 247 runs in 110 minutes until Holmes declared at 1 p.m. with the score on 706 for 4, the highest total ever recorded against Nottinghamshire. To this day it is the highest score by Surrey away from The Oval. The score of 194 by David Fletcher, then twenty-two years old, was the highest of his career.

Following the early wickets of Harris and Simpson, both to Eric Bedser, Keeton and Hardstaff came together to bat out the match to a draw on a wicket that was a dream for batsmen and had been a bed of despair for the Nottinghamshire bowlers.

'The Four Centurions', Errol Holmes, Jack Parker, Stan Squires and David Fletcher.

SURREY v. NOTTINGHAMSHIRE

Played at Trent Bridge on 24th, 26th and 27th May 1947 [3-day Match]   Toss: Nottinghamshire
Match drawn

NOTTINGHAMSHIRE

W.W. Keeton	b A.V. Bedser	59	c Parker b A.V. Bedser		64
C.B. Harris	lbw b Watts	30	c A.V. Bedser b E.A. Bedser		16
R.T. Simpson	c McIntyre b A.V. Bedser	33	lbw b E.A. Bedser		0
J. Hardstaff	b E.A. Bedser	65	c & b Squires		85
F.W. Stocks	c Watts b Squires	19	not out		19
T.B. Reddick	b E.A. Bedser	44	not out		8
*W.A. Sime	b A.V. Bedser	47			
W. Voce	b A.V. Bedser	24			
H.J. Butler	not out	35			
A. Jepson	b Gover	13			
#E.A. Meads	c McIntyre b E.A. Bedser	7			
Extras	b 15, lb 9, nb 1	25	b 5, lb 3, nb 1		9
Total	**(all out)**	**401**	**(for 4 wickets)**		**201**

SURREY

E.A. Bedser	b Jepson	12
D.G.W. Fletcher	b Butler	194
R.J. Gregory	lbw b Voce	87
H.S. Squires	c Stocks b Butler	154
J.F. Parker	not out	108
*E.R.T. Holmes	not out	122
#A.J.W. McIntyre		
E.A. Watts		
A.V. Bedser		
A.R. Gover		
T.H. Barling		
Extras	b 13, lb 16	29
Total	**(for 4 wickets declared)**	**706**

Bowling

SURREY	O	M	R	W	O	M	R	W
Gover	31	8	79	1	12	1	31	0
A.V. Bedser	30	6	79	4	15	4	35	1
Watts	24	3	76	1	3	0	13	0
Parker	15	3	31	0	9	0	21	0
E.A. Bedser	16.3	1	55	3	12	3	28	2
Squires	22	4	56	1	16	1	64	1

NOTTINGHAMSHIRE	O	M	R	W
Butler	46	6	150	2
Jepson	33	4	135	1
Voce	30	6	93	1
Stocks	15	0	84	0
Harris	16	0	91	0
Sime	16	1	71	0
Reddick	6	0	34	0
Hardstaff	4	0	19	0

FALL OF WICKETS

	N	S	N
1st	64	25	46
2nd	131	180	46
3rd	134	459	136
4th	186	459	188
5th	261	–	–
6th	266	–	–
7th	320	–	–
8th	349	–	–
9th	378	–	–
10th	401	–	–

Umpires: C.F. Root and C.N. Woolley

Surrey v. Lancashire

Date: 9-11 June 1948   County Championship
Location: The Oval

Lancashire lacked a bowler of real pace in this match but forced the Surrey batsmen to work hard for their runs on a good pitch. A stubborn first-wicket stand by Fishlock and Fletcher saw them take two hours forty-five minutes to accumulate 115 runs with Fishlock taking two hours over his first 43 runs. In an effort to force the pace the Surrey captain, Errol Holmes, changed the batting order to little avail as the home side finished the day on 250 for the loss of 8 wickets.

The Surrey innings closed on the second day after a total of seven hours' batting. Stuart Surridge struck early, taking 2 wickets for 9 runs in his opening spell but then Winston Place and Jack Ikin added 58 for the third wicket in an hour. Place alone showed enough ability to cope with a keen attack, taking two hours thirty-five minutes for his 51, but the follow-on was averted with the ninth pair together. In their second innings Surrey lost Fishlock and Squires quickly but by the close of play had stretched their lead to172 with 8 wickets in hand.

An inspired spell of bowling by the Lancashire captain, Ken Cranston, and a gallant innings by Place had victory in their grasp but they faltered in the last half hour to lose the match by 1 run. Cranston's bowling in the morning had most of the Surrey batsmen in difficulties on an easy paced pitch but Surridge was always ready to strike the ball violently. At one stage Cranston had taken 4 wickets for 12 runs and with Richard Pollard keeping a good length from the other end Surrey were dismissed for a meagre total of 123. Surridge and Eric Bedser then set about the early Lancashire batsmen and had 5 of them back in the pavilion with 119 runs on the board. Place, however, remained imperturbable and needed a partner. Alan Wharton suggested he was the man and by 5.45 p.m. the score was passing 200 when victory seemed assured as both were batting and running between the wickets well. Place, having scored thirteen fours in his 120, was then smartly run out by Stan Squires. Howard came in obviously intent on a quick finish and fell to a great catch in the deep by McMahon off Eric Bedser. Bill Roberts was then smartly caught at the wicket by McIntyre but Pollard and Malcolm Hilton seemed comfortable until three minutes from the end of allocated time. Hilton hit out at Bedser and was caught at the third attempt by Laurie Fishlock at long off. A great game lost and won.

All-round strength provided the basis of Surrey's success during the 1948 season in finishing runners-up, 4 points behind Glamorgan, in the County Championship. Although never heading the table, Surrey, after a moderate start, kept well within reach of the leaders. Hopes of winning the competition ran high when the side met Glamorgan at Cardiff in mid-August, but defeat in two days by an innings and a similar reverse in the next match against Middlesex deprived them of chief honours. However, the basis of the team that was so successful in the 1950s was coming together.

Laurie Fishlock batting against Kent in 1951.

SURREY v. LANCASHIRE

Played at The Oval on 9th, 10th and 11th June 1948 [3-day Match]   Toss: Surrey
Surrey won by 1 run

SURREY

L.B. Fishlock	b Roberts	78	c Ikin b Cranston		1
D.G.W. Fletcher	b Pollard	50	c Howard b Cranston		24
W.S. Surridge	b Cranston	0	[10] c Roberts b Pollard		29
*E.R.T. Holmes	b Roberts	26	[8] b Cranston		1
H.S. Squires	st E.H. Edrich b Roberts	6	[3] c G.A. Edrich b Cranston		6
H.T. Barling	c E.H. Edrich b Hilton	35	[4] b Pollard		24
M.R. Barton	run out	32	[5] c Pollard b Cranston		3
J.F. Parker	b Roberts	7	[6] b Cranston		10
#A.J.W. McIntyre	not out	45	[7] b Pollard		1
E.A. Bedser	c & b Cranston	17	[9] c Brierley b Cranston		12
J.W.J. McMahon	c Ikin b Cranston	0	not out		8
Extras	lb 2, w 1, nb 1	4	lb 3, nb 1		4
Total	**(all out)**	**300**	**(all out)**		**123**

LANCASHIRE

W. Place	b McMahon	51	run out		120
T.L. Brierley	c Fletcher b Surridge	6	lbw b Surridge		17
G.A. Edrich	c McIntyre b Surridge	2	c McIntyre b Surridge		3
J.T. Ikin	c Surridge b Bedser	33	c Parker b Bedser		7
#E.H. Edrich	lbw b Bedser	8	lbw b Surridge		27
A. Wharton	run out	11	[6] b Bedser		46
N.D. Howard	not out	29	[8] c McMahon b Bedser		19
*K. Cranston	c McMahon b Bedser	7	[6] c McIntyre b Bedser		0
R. Pollard	c Bedser b McMahon	10	not out		3
W.B. Roberts	b McMahon	13	c McIntyre b Squires		1
M.J. Hilton	c Squires b McMahon	1	c Fishlock b Bedser		1
Extras	b 3, nb 1, w 1	5	lb 1, nb 1		2
Total	**(all out)**	**176**	**(all out)**		**246**

Bowling

LANCASHIRE	O	M	R	W	O	M	R	W
Pollard	36	11	75	1	26	8	56	3
Cranston	20.4	6	39	3	23.1	7	43	7
Roberts	48	20	64	4	5	0	13	0
Wharton	9	0	33	0				
Hilton	35	11	67	1	3	2	7	0
Ikin	7	1	18	0				

SURREY	O	M	R	W	O	M	R	W
Surridge	11	3	37	3	23	5	71	3
Parker	11	7	9	0	15	2	35	0
McMahon	20.3	6	46	4	13	1	49	0
Bedser	23	4	68	3	22.5	1	75	5
Squires	8	2	11	0	6	2	14	1

FALL OF WICKETS

	S	L	S	L
1st	115	8	4	30
2nd	116	14	12	50
3rd	156	72	51	66
4th	163	88	59	116
5th	164	112	71	119
6th	207	116	72	216
7th	216	131	73	232
8th	249	144	75	241
9th	300	174	113	243
10th	300	176	123	246

Umpires: H.G. Baldwin and A. Skelding

Surrey v. Kent

Date: 12, 14-15 July 1952   **County Championship**
Location: The Oval

The appointment of a new captain coincided with a transformation of Surrey cricket and they won the Championship outright for the first time since 1914 entirely by merit. Such was Surrey's strength, they did not concede any points (4 points being awarded for leading on first innings) until 13 June, when Glamorgan led them on first innings at Llanelli, and not until 18 July were their colours lowered for the first time, by Lancashire. On that occasion, at The Oval, and also when they were beaten away by Warwickshire and Yorkshire, they were without Alec Bedser, Laker, May and Lock, who were engaged on Test duty.

One reason for Surrey's tremendous advance was the confident assurance of all the players in their own ability, and for that happy frame of mind they had to thank Stuart Surridge. He believed in playing attacking cricket at all the time, and when occasionally things did not go well he was content to take the responsibility. That the Surrey batsmen hit off runs in the fourth innings on a worn pitch when there would have been every excuse for an inept display was because Surridge insisted that from the start they must try to knock the bowlers off their length.

While capable batting is essential, brilliance in the field usually decides the Championship. This was certainly the case with Surrey. They possessed three England bowlers in Alec Bedser, Laker and Lock, who

Peter May strikes out against Kent in 1959 with Godfrey Evans keeping wicket.

Above left: Tom Clark.

Above right: Stuart Surridge – the most successful Surrey captain of all time.

made the attack undeniably the best in the country. On top of this, the fielding under the inspiring example of Surridge can seldom have been surpassed. He set up a new Surrey record by holding 58 catches, and Lock took 54. Anywhere close to the bat suited Surridge, and by his watchfulness, anticipation and agility he pounced on almost seemingly impossible chances.

In this match, although not as strongly supported in the field as they could have expected, the Surrey opening bowlers, Surridge and Alec Bedser, justified the captain's action in giving Kent first innings on a damp pitch by sharing all 10 wickets that fell for 192, a total that Surrey answered with 46 for 2 wickets at the close on the first day. In taking 7 for 80 Surridge achieved his second-best analysis in first-class cricket. Moreover, Kent's two highest scorers were missed off him at first slip, Shirreff when 39, and Edrich when 38. Otherwise, Surridge was as lucky as Bedser was unlucky. Not only did several Kent batsmen precipitate their own downfall by ill-judged or reckless strokes, but the end to which Surridge bowled remained awkward much longer. Bedser began by dismissing Fagg in his first over – after two unsuccessful appeals – and he broke the back of the batting by taking 3 of the first 4 wickets, Surridge followed with the last 6. Two men batted for Kent as the situation demanded. For three hours Shirreff watched the ball carefully and picked out the correct ball to hit. Brian Edrich, who returned to the side following an absence of eight games through a broken finger, defended well, in spite of another painful blow on the same finger.

SURREY v. KENT

Next day Surrey made 325 to establish a first-innings lead of 133 runs. Naturally, with Surrey's fine display during the season, there was a large attendance, but there must have been more than a few who would not have come had it not been for the first appearance in the season for the county of Peter May. His supporters were right. He made 124, rich in strokes of every kind played in every direction, which stamped him as a batsman of the highest quality. He had to contend with good fast bowling by Page, intelligent attack from Dovey and Shirreff, and the spin of Wright, bowling with a shorter run. Against this he never looked in difficulty. He was a complete master of the bowling, and before edging, perhaps wearily, the ball to the wicketkeeper he had made his first hundred at The Oval.

If all paled before this, he had able assistance from McIntyre, and afterwards Laker showed himself as an all-rounder of merit. Godfrey Evans steered Kent to what might have been safety after the loss of 2 wickets. His many strokes to the off-side as well as clever leg-side play rewarded him with 65 not out, and his partner, O'Linn, was 19 not out at the close of the second day, when Kent were 106 for 2.

On the last day Surrey were set 188 to win in ninety-two minutes and they succeeded by means of a series of short but sharp forcing innings by various of their batsmen. There can be no question of Kent being kind, for when the tea interval came with 8 of their wickets down they went on batting for a few minutes afterwards before declaring with nine men out, thus forcing another interval of ten minutes, which meant two runs a minute and a bit more for Surrey to score. In the morning Evans went on to score 92, having been hit severely on the hand by Surridge's faster ball, and when he was out he retired from the match. His overnight partner, O'Linn, even exceeded him in scoring, completing 100, but it took him much longer – not far short of five hours – and even allowing for Kent's only object being to save the game, there was too much of the dead bat to the pitched-up ball on a batsman's pitch.

Surrey's effort to score fast was clear from the start. Eric Bedser hit out strongly but was first out, leaving May to join Fletcher. May, whose 29 was by far the best innings, showed how a classic stylist can adapt himself in forcing the pace if needs be. When May chased a wide one and was caught at the wicket by O'Linn, who standing back proved a good deputy for Evans, Constable carried on the good work, with Fletcher, though never missing a chance of scoring, being content to be second string to his partners. But the steady bowling of Page and Shirreff, with a defensive field, told its tale, and Surrey, with wickets falling, were well behind the clock. They had 122 to make with an hour to go. But when Fletcher, the top scorer, was out when he had made 52 with only twenty minutes to go the Surrey total was 125 for 6, which meant 63 more to get. Alec Bedser, with some lusty hitting, gave Surrey a slight ray of hope, but there were 44 runs to be made in a bare fourteen minutes. Not impossible, but unlikely. Surridge, however, was just the man for such an occasion. He hit hard and he kept his head as a captain should. The score mounted rapidly and, when the umpires decreed that there should be just one more over, there were but 2 runs to get. Surridge took charge and struck the second ball to the off-side boundary. So marked was the tension in the final minutes that the crowd rose to their feet and a burst of cheering broke out as he made the winning hit with the clock pointing to a shade after half-past six.

SURREY v. KENT

Played at The Oval on 12th, 14th and 15th July 1952 [3-day Match]   Toss: Surrey
Surrey won by 2 wickets

KENT

A.E. Fagg	c McIntyre b A.V. Bedser	0	c Parker b A.V. Bedser	10
A.H. Phebey	b A.V. Bedser	29	lbw b Surridge	3
#T.G. Evans	c McIntyre b Surridge	9	st McIntyre b A.V. Bedser	92
S. O'Linn	b A.V. Bedser	3	not out	111
A.C. Shirreff	b Surridge	75	lbw b Laker	20
R. Mayes	b Surridge	11	c McIntyre b A.V. Bedser	5
B.R. Edrich	c McIntyre b Surridge	41	lbw b Lock	31
*W. Murray-Wood	c Lock b Surridge	0	c May b Constable	4
R.R. Dovey	b Surridge	2	b A.V. Bedser	0
D.V.P. Wright	not out	8	lbw b Lock	4
J.C.T. Page	c Parker b Surridge	9	not out	5
Extras	lb 3, nb 2	5	b 21, lb 9, nb 5	35
Total	**(all out)**	**192**	**(for 9 wickets declared)**	**320**

SURREY

E.A. Bedser	lbw b Page	3	c O'Linn b Page	20
D.G.W. Fletcher	c Fagg b Page	12	c & b Shirreff	52
P.B.H. May	c Evans b Dovey	124	c O'Linn b Page	29
B. Constable	b Dovey	22	c O'Linn b Page	17
J.F. Parker	c Mayes b Wright	19	b Page	1
T.H. Clark	c Fagg b Dovey	42	not out	24
#A.J.W. McIntyre	c O'Linn b Dovey	43	c & b Shirreff	0
J.C. Laker	c Fagg b Dovey	23	c & b Shirreff	15
A.V. Bedser	b Dovey	3	b Shirreff	14
*W.S. Surridge	c Mayes b Dovey	14	not out	16
G.A.R. Lock	not out	15		
Extras	b 1, lb 4	5	lb 1, nb 1	2
Total	**(all out)**	**325**	**(for 8 wickets)**	**190**

Bowling

SURREY	O	M	R	W	O	M	R	W
A.V. Bedser	32	9	67	3	35	6	89	4
Surridge	30.2	7	80	7	27	5	73	1
Laker	9	2	21	0	29	11	50	1
Lock	22	14	19	0	19	1	56	2
E.A. Bedser					11	5	9	0
Constable					6	2	8	1

KENT	O	M	R	W	O	M	R	W
Page	27	2	105	2	11	0	48	4
Shirreff	31	5	83	0	15	0	106	4
Wright	16	4	50	1				
Dovey	31.1	5	82	7	4.2	0	34	0

FALL OF WICKETS

	K	S	K	S
1st	0	5	12	29
2nd	13	36	48	75
3rd	18	74	143	95
4th	69	122	182	97
5th	100	205	194	104
6th	143	262	275	125
7th	147	275	288	144
8th	153	278	291	162
9th	176	297	320	–
10th	192	325	–	–

Umpires: E. Cooke and K. McCanlis

SURREY v. MIDDLESEX

Date: 9, 11-12 August 1952   **County Championship**
Location: The Oval

Owing to rain the match did not begin until 12.15 p.m. on Monday and then, although the ball seldom lifted, bowlers generally held the upper hand. Sixteen wickets fell in the day on a damp wicket. Middlesex were bowled out for 77 in less than two-and-three-quarter hours. Middlesex had never recovered from a depressing start. From the moment when Thompson, playing too soon at Alec Bedser's disguised slower pace, gave mid-on a simple catch they were in trouble. From 7 for 1 they went to 16 for 4 in less than an hour, a violent spasm that saw Robertson brilliantly caught one-handed and low down by McIntyre behind the wicket, Edrich bowled by a great ball from Surridge and Brown leg before wicket to the same bowler with one that went the other way.

But for Compton, Knightley-Smith and later Bennett the situation could have been a lot worse. Compton was at the crease for fifty minutes at the height of the crisis trying to impress his personality on the bowlers. Knightley-Smith, a stylish left-hander, helped Compton in a useful little stand that ended with another of Lock's miraculous low catches at backward short leg off Bedser. Compton's leg glide was legitimate and played right off the face of the bat, but Lock's dive to the left turned the situation. Knightley-Smith added two neat on-drives off Surridge, each for four, before Laker finally arrived to have him taken at the wicket after an hour, attempting a big hit. Of the rest, only Bennett showed any resistance. He battled away bravely for just over an hour, and finally died a hero's death in what, for such a day, was a flurry of fours.

Yet Surrey were to fare only slightly better when they came to the wicket at a quarter to four. Fletcher

Alec Bedser.

went, hanging out his bat, before tea to Warr. But Eric Bedser saw his chance before the effect of the roller wore off, forcing what runs he could out of the lively pace of Warr and Moss, and once claiming a five, all run, off an on-drive. It was none too soon, for immediately after the interval the sun arrived to sharpen up the pitch, and almost at once Moss brought a ball back violently to hit Bedser's leg stump. Moss, indeed, now bowled really well for a spell, but Fishlock, surviving chances at 1 and at 32 was in an aggressive mood. These lost chances, indeed, underlined the difference between the sides. Fishlock and May, who batted with all his quiet assurance, fashioned a most valuable third-wicket stand of 45 that took Surrey well within reach of their opponents. But the last three-quarters of an hour saw some fine left-arm spin bowling by Young and a remarkable catch by Warr to dismiss Parker put Middlesex back in the running, even though May still remained to put Surrey into the lead.

The last day comprised three major phases, each of different character. Young claimed the last 3 Surrey wickets to earn him figures of 6 for 42, and with a lead

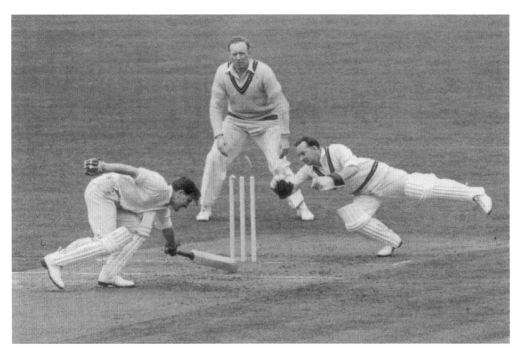

Arthur McIntyre attempting to stump Doug Insole in the match against Essex in 1951.

of 52 Surridge declared at 12.15 p.m. So with just over an hour left to lunch the vital central pattern to the affair was begun. The way Robertson and Thompson began left the impression that they were after a declaration and a final onslaught themselves on Surrey. Robertson in particular batted freely and elegantly. After only 2 overs each Bedser and Surridge made way for Laker and Lock, and in just over half an hour 33 runs were added to the total. This was good cricket by any standards. But then the picture changed in a trice as the effect of the roller wore off. From that moment Middlesex fought for mere survival, and not until a bright and highly important half-hour after tea between Compton and Young, when 40 runs were added, did they emerge from the shadows. Their troubles began when Thompson, carrying his exuberance too far, leapt down the wicket to Laker only to lose his off stump. Soon 33 for 1 had become 41 for 3 when Edrich was swiftly taken in Laker's leg-trap on the forward stretch and Robertson bowled by Lock's faster ball, one that also kept low. It was at the fall of Edrich's wicket at 1.15 p.m. that Compton began his fighting act of rescue. All through the afternoon, until 5.10 p.m. when Moss was finally bowled by Bedser, Compton fought the spin of Laker and Lock with all the skill and experience at his command. He was certainly fortunate at times, particularly with the left-handed Lock, who must have been perilously near more than once with lbw appeals, while on occasion he did his best to run himself out. But it was a great and intriguing battle, though some stupid and ill-mannered people at times paraded their lack of appreciation of the situation by ironic clapping. Had Compton gone Surrey would have been home by a street.

At tea Middlesex were 112 for 8, 3 of the wickets having melted away in the last quarter of an hour before the interval as soon as Laker returned to the Pavilion End. With just under two hours left and only 2

Surrey v. Middlesex

Laurie Fishlock.

wickets remaining Middlesex, in fact, were no more than 60 to the good. Thus was the value of Compton's performance set in its true perspective. But now in the half-hour after tea Young came to join him in a lively stand of 41. This seemed to drain Surrey's chance away until, at last, with the 150 just passed, Bedser returned to finish off in 1 over the splendid work of Laker and Lock, who had spun away for most of the time on a quieter but still responsive wicket. It is interesting here to remark that Surridge never claimed the new ball, although available at 100 for 5. So Compton, applauded by his opponents, retired unbeaten just short of his fifty after batting for two hours and fifty-five minutes.

Now, with seventy minutes left, Surrey set about their task against the pace of Moss and Warr. At once they were ahead of the clock as Eric Bedser helped himself to four firm boundaries before being yorked by Moss. Shortly after Fishlock arrived Fletcher was bowled trying to hook Warr off the middle stump. But now Fishlock and May strode gloriously home. In just over half an hour they gathered in the last 60 runs. Straight drives, cuts and pulls flowed freely; short runs disrupted the Middlesex plan and sometimes even brought overthrows, a stroke by Fishlock past extra cover counting five in this way. So were Moss and Warr cut to pieces, for Young was used hardly at all. The crowd was on its feet as boundary followed boundary, and it was somehow right that Fishlock, with seven fours and a five in his 41 in even time, should be the one to send the figures on the scoreboard singing beyond the victory mark with one last vicious hook off Moss.

SURREY *v.* MIDDLESEX

Played at The Oval on 9th, 11th and 12th August 1952 [3-day Match]   Toss: Middlesex
Surrey won by 8 wickets

MIDDLESEX

J.D.B. Robertson	c McIntyre b A.V. Bedser	6	b Lock		27
A.W. Thompson	c Fletcher b A.V. Bedser	6	b Laker		13
*W.J. Edrich	b Surridge	2	c Surridge b Laker		1
D.C.S. Compton	c Lock b A.V. Bedser	9	not out		43
S.M. Brown	lbw b Surridge	1	c & b Lock		14
W. Knightley-Smith	c McIntyre b Laker	16	lbw b Lock		11
D. Bennett	c E.A. Bedser b Laker	20	b Laker		6
#L.H. Compton	c Clark b Lock	7	c Lock b Laker		1
J.J. Warr	b Lock	0	c Surridge b Lock		0
J.A. Young	not out	7	b A.V. Bedser		22
A.E. Moss	st McIntyre b Lock	0	b A.V. Bedser		0
Extras	b 2, lb 1	3	b 8, lb 6		14
Total	**(all out)**	**77**	**(all out)**		**152**

SURREY

E.A. Bedser	b Moss	16	b Moss		19
D.G.W. Fletcher	c Edrich b Warr	1	b Warr		15
L.B. Fishlock	c Moss b Young	33	not out		41
P.B.H. May	st L.H. Compton b Young	31	not out		24
J.F. Parker	c Warr b Bennett	0			
T.H. Clark	b Young	13			
#A.J.W. McIntyre	c Edrich b Young	0			
J.C. Laker	c Robertson b Young	20			
*W.S. Surridge	c L.H. Compton b Young	8			
A.V. Bedser	not out	4			
G.A.R. Lock					
Extras	b 2, lb 1	3	lb 3		3
Total	**(for 9 wickets declared)**	**129**	**(for 2 wickets)**		**102**

Bowling

SURREY	O	M	R	W	O	M	R	W
A.V. Bedser	18	9	17	3	15	4	24	2
Surridge	15	2	25	2	2	0	12	0
Laker	10	3	20	2	33	14	50	4
Lock	7.5	4	12	3	31	15	47	4
E.A. Bedser					4	2	5	0

MIDDLESEX	O	M	R	W	O	M	R	W
Warr	13	4	23	1	6	0	39	1
Moss	19	8	32	1	10.5	0	51	1
Young	18.5	8	42	6	4	1	9	0
Bennett	8	1	25	1				
D.C.S. Compton	1	0	4	0				

FALL OF WICKETS

	M	S	M	S
1st	7	9	33	26
2nd	14	21	41	42
3rd	14	66	41	–
4th	16	67	57	–
5th	30	89	86	–
6th	46	89	106	–
7th	57	106	108	–
8th	57	120	111	–
9th	75	129	152	–
10th	77	–	152	–

Umpires: F. Chester and E. Cooke

SURREY v. WARWICKSHIRE

Date: 16 May 1953   **County Championship**
Location: The Oval

Remarkable cricket took place on a rain-damaged pitch at The Oval as Surrey beat Warwickshire by an innings and 49 runs in one day.

Members rose as one when the triumphant Surrey team walked from the field having begun their Championship programme with this memorable victory. The last and only time that a first-class match had been completed in one day at The Oval was in 1857, when Julius Caesar was the Surrey opening batsman. Surrey have been involved in three other matches that finished in one day, against MCC and Ground at Lord's in 1872, against Lancashire at Old Trafford in 1888 and against Leicestershire at Leicester in 1897.

The heroes for Surrey were Alec Bedser and Jim Laker. Bedser bowled magnificently when play commenced at noon. Unable to obtain a proper foothold on the wet turf, he attacked the leg stump at below normal pace and equalled his best performance of 8 for 18 in the first innings, helped by great catching from Lock, Laker and Fletcher in the leg trap. He followed this by taking 4 wickets for 17 in the second innings, so finishing with a match analysis of 12 for 35.

Surrey also found the pitch treacherous but, chiefly through a sound innings by Constable, they took the lead with only 2 wickets down. The score then went from 50 for 2 to 81 for 7, and only the aggressiveness of Surridge, who hit three sixes in 4 balls from Hollies, Laker, who drove Grove out of the ground and Lock enabled them to gain a substantial lead. Lock became the second-highest scorer before, while hitting out valiantly in a last-wicket stand, he was struck on the head by the ball and was taken to hospital with a gash near the right eye. Fortunately no serious injury resulted, but it meant his retirement from the match.

Laker was called into the attack for the first time when Warwickshire batted again and began the final rout by achieving a hat-trick. This was the first hat-trick of the season and the second of Laker's career. He dismissed Spooner, Dollery and Hitchcock while the total went from 26 for 2 to 26 for 5.

Warwickshire were dismissed at their first attempt in one hour fifteen minutes for 45 runs with only Spooner reaching double figures. This, not surprisingly, was the lowest total so far of that season. Dismissed

Alec Bedser.

for 52 in the second innings in one hour ten minutes, Taylor and Grove were the only batsmen to score more than 10 runs. Altogether, ten of their batsmen in the match were dismissed without scoring. Although 29 wickets fell during the day for 243 runs, not once during either Warwickshire innings did a Surrey bowler hit the stumps, sixteen Warwickshire batsmen being caught, a fact that emphasised Surrey's excellent fielding. The match, which had started late, finished at 6.40 p.m., ten minutes after normal time had been reached and extra time claimed by Surrey with their rivals 49 for 7 in their second innings. Altogether forty-five minutes were lost through weather during the day's play.

Alec Bedser enjoyed a great season in 1953, taking 162 wickets at an average of 16.67 and performing well in the Test matches against Australia. Bedser took 100 wickets in a season eleven times. Having first played for the county in 1939 one wonders how many more wickets than his career total of 1,459 he would have taken but for the loss of six seasons due to the Second World War.

SURREY *v.* WARWICKSHIRE

Played at The Oval on 16th May 1953 [3-day Match]
Surrey won by an innings and 49 runs

Toss: Not known

WARWICKSHIRE

F.C. Gardner	c Laker b A.V. Bedser	7	c Laker b A.V. Bedser	7
T.W. Cartwright	lbw b A.V. Bedser	0	lbw b Laker	9
D.D. Taylor	c Fletcher b A.V. Bedser	0	lbw b A.V. Bedser	20
#R.T. Spooner	c Whittaker b A.V. Bedser	16	c & b Laker	0
*H.E. Dollery	c Lock b A.V. Bedser	8	c Surridge b Laker	0
R.E. Hitchcock	c Whittaker b Lock	3	c A.V. Bedser b Laker	0
A. Townsend	c McIntyre b Lock	7	run out	0
R.T. Weeks	not out	0	c Surridge b A.V. Bedser	0
C.W.C. Grove	c Fletcher b A.V. Bedser	3	c Constable b Laker	10
K.R. Dollery	c Brazier b A.V. Bedser	0	not out	0
W.E. Hollies	c Laker b A.V. Bedser	0	c sub b A.V. Bedser	0
Extras	lb 1	1	b 2, lb 3, nb 1	6
Total	**(all out)**	**45**	**(all out)**	**52**

SURREY

E.A. Bedser	b K.R. Dollery	5
D.G.W. Fletcher	c Townsend b Weeks	13
B. Constable	c Grove b K.R. Dollery	37
T.H. Clark	c K.R. Dollery b Hollies	2
A.F. Brazier	c Townsend b Hollies	6
G.J. Whittaker	b K.R. Dollery	0
#A.J.W. McIntyre	c & b K.R. Dollery	9
J.C. Laker	c H.E. Dollery b Hollies	18
*W.S. Surridge	b Grove	19
A.V. Bedser	not out	5
G.A.R. Lock	retired hurt	27
Extras	lb 4, nb 1	5
Total	**(all out)**	**146**

Bowling

SURREY	O	M	R	W	O	M	R	W
A.V. Bedser	13.5	4	18	8	13.4	7	17	4
Surridge	6	1	17	0				
Lock	7	3	9	2				
Laker					13	6	29	5

WARWICKSHIRE	O	M	R	W
Grove	10.1	3	29	1
K.R. Dollery	11	4	40	4
Weeks	8	1	24	1
Hollies	10	4	48	3

FALL OF WICKETS

	W	S	W
1st	3	5	20
2nd	3	27	22
3rd	8	50	26
4th	27	61	26
5th	30	65	26
6th	36	77	32
7th	42	81	32
8th	45	108	49
9th	45	119	52
10th	45	—	52

Umpires: E. Cooke and L.H. Gray

Surrey v. Lancashire

Date: 30 May, 1-2 June 1953   **County Championship**
Location: Old Trafford

This was possibly the Champions' best performance of the season. In any case it went a long way towards them winning the title again, for Lancashire pressed them close for so many weeks. Their success did not come with the same ease as in 1952. They lost the lead on 11 June and found the challenges of Sussex, Lancashire, Leicestershire and Middlesex so keen that they did not regain it until 25 August. Early in the season it was plain that the batting was suffering from the loss of the experience and enterprise of Fishlock and Parker, who had retired. Although May, now down from Cambridge, was available from the beginning of the summer, he did not find his best form immediately, and not until Subba Row joined the side after the Varsity match did the middle batting become more stable.

At Old Trafford, honours were about even on the first day in Jack Ikin's benefit match, which was watched by about 10,000 people. An opening stand of 63 between Washbrook and Ikin gave rise to hopes of a big home total, but after lunch 4 wickets fell quickly for 51 runs, and it was not until Edrich and Wharton became partners that the accurate Surrey bowling wilted. Wharton showed his colleague how Lock and Alec Bedser should be played. In eighty minutes 88 runs were put on for the sixth wicket before Wharton was out to a brilliant diving catch by Lock in Bedser's leg trap. In a three-hour stay Edrich went on to score 77 before falling to Lock. Until the sixth-wicket pair set about the bowling, Lock had been particularly impressive. In a two-and-a-half hour spell, Lock had figures of 29-17-39-2 and he finished with 5 for 89. The Surrey fielding was brilliant before tea, but afterwards Surridge, Alec Bedser and Whittaker missed simple chances.

On the second day, May showed a return to form. His off-side strokes were particularly good and brought him most of the thirteen boundaries in his valuable 75. The merit of his innings extended beyond his own contribution, since it had an inspiring effect on the remaining batsmen, who found there was nothing wrong with the pitch. In succession Clark, Whittaker and McIntyre helped May in partnerships over 50 and Surrey did splendidly to obtain a first-innings lead of 28 after half the side had been out for 49. McIntyre, last out, was particularly severe on the Lancashire attack, which never equalled the standard set by Surrey. Lancashire had a disastrous fifty-five minutes at the close, losing Washbrook, Ikin and Place, all to brilliant catches, for only 28.

Eric Bedser batting v. Middlesex with Leslie Compton keeping wicket and Bill Edrich at first slip.

On the last day 7 Lancashire second innings wickets fell for 42. Alec Bedser and Surridge were in great form on a lively pitch and brilliantly supported by Lock at short leg. Surrey's triumphant march was again held up by Wharton, who found an unexpected ally in Hilton. Between them they carried the score to 104 before Wharton was caught behind the wicket by Constable, deputising for McIntyre, who had a damaged finger. Hilton went on to reach a gallant fifty. Last out at 130, he played the bowling with far more enterprise and determination than his predecessors.

Surrey, set to make 103, lost Fletcher to Statham with only 3 runs on the board, but Eric Bedser and Constable hit 95 in an hour. Although Bedser was run out for an excellent 59 Surrey won comfortably and deservedly.

SURREY *v.* LANCASHIRE

Played at Old Trafford on 30th May, 1st and 2nd June 1953 [3-day Match]   Toss: Lancashire
Surrey won by 8 wickets

LANCASHIRE

C. Washbrook	c McIntyre b A.V. Bedser	45	c Lock b A.V. Bedser	6
J.T. Ikin	c McIntyre b Lock	25	c A.V. Bedser b Surridge	12
W. Place	run out	5	c Lock b A.V. Bedser	4
G.A. Edrich	c E.A. Bedser b Lock	77	c Surridge b A.V. Bedser	0
K.J. Grieves	lbw b Lock	8	c Lock b Surridge	7
*N.D. Howard	c Lock b Laker	6	c Lock b Surridge	0
A. Wharton	c Lock b A.V. Bedser	46	c Constable b Surridge	26
M.J. Hilton	c McIntyre b Lock	0	c Laker b A.V. Bedser	56
#F.D. Parr	b Laker	24	c Lock b A.V. Bedser	10
R. Tattersall	c Fletcher b Lock	4	c Fletcher b Surridge	1
J.B. Statham	not out	1	not out	2
Extras	b 10, lb 4	14	b 1, lb 3, nb 2	6
Total	**(all out)**	**255**	**(all out)**	**130**

SURREY

A.V. Bedser	c & b Tattersall	0		
*W.S. Surridge	c Place b Tattersall	29		
E.A. Bedser	run out	5	[1] run out	59
D.G.W. Fletcher	lbw b Hilton	0	[2] c Edrich b Statham	3
B. Constable	c Grieves b Tattersall	6	[3] not out	33
P.B.H. May	b Statham	75	[4] not out	5
T.H. Clark	c Parr b Hilton	39		
G.J. Whittaker	lbw b Grieves	30		
#A.J.W. McIntyre	b Statham	76		
J.C. Laker	b Statham	15		
G.A.R. Lock	not out	0		
Extras	b 8	8	lb 3	3
Total	**(all out)**	**283**	**(for 2 wickets)**	**103**

Bowling

SURREY	O	M	R	W	O	M	R	W
A.V. Bedser	30	9	49	2	25.2	4	62	5
Surridge	17	5	42	0	21	3	46	5
Lock	45	20	89	5	4	1	16	0
Laker	26.3	9	61	2				

LANCASHIRE	O	M	R	W	O	M	R	W
Tattersall	27	7	77	3	4	0	25	0
Wharton	5	1	22	0	7	1	17	0
Statham	14	3	47	3	7	1	27	1
Hilton	38	10	106	2	6	3	24	0
Grieves	9	3	23	1	1.4	0	7	0

FALL OF WICKETS

	L	S	L	S
1st	63	1	17	3
2nd	80	26	22	98
3rd	80	29	24	–
4th	91	37	28	–
5th	114	49	39	–
6th	202	113	39	–
7th	207	177	43	–
8th	236	232	104	–
9th	253	258	118	–
10th	255	283	130	–

Umpires: E. Cooke and W.T. Jones

SURREY v. NOTTINGHAMSHIRE

Date: 1, 3-4 August 1953   **County Championship**
Location: The Oval

On the Saturday when the pitch was sodden and much time was lost, Surrey concentrated on defence, but the sun shone on the last two days when both teams played grand cricket. May played two fine innings for Surrey and Simpson and Clay gave Nottinghamshire a fine start to their first innings. Finally, Surrey owed much to the tenacious bowling of Lock. Between the start and tea, during which 185 minutes' play was possible, Surrey batted laboriously to score 130 runs. May was dropped off Dooland when 37, but he continued to gather quick runs, mostly by means of the cover-drive. By the close he and Constable had put on 115. Earlier Fletcher and Clark opened with a stand of 75 before Clark was brilliantly stumped as he went forward to drive. In a little over an hour Fletcher and May put on 51 for the second wicket. Fletcher, next out, was caught at mid-wicket. He batted three hours for his 61, made out of 126.

On the second morning May completed 135 not out in four hours twenty minutes. He shared in stands of 120 with Constable and 82 unfinished with Eric Bedser as Surridge declared. Simpson and Clay, punished the Surrey attack, taking only two-and-a-quarter hours to put on 159. So keenly did they attack the bowling that at one stage it took them only an hour to compile 104. Nevertheless, Laker and Lock, the two bowlers who came in for the most punishment, had their revenge. They started a Nottinghamshire collapse and their good work was followed up by Alec Bedser and Surridge using the new ball. Trouble started when Simpson stumbled playing forward to Lock and was stumped. Clay, third out at 182, scored one more run than his captain, but he had batted three-quarters of an hour longer. It was after his departure that Nottinghamshire collapsed, although lusty hitting by Butler staved off the end. On the last morning their first innings came to an end and Surrey made quick runs before declaring again.

In one of the most exciting finishes of the season, Surrey set Nottinghamshire to make 209 in 135 minutes, the rate being 93 runs an hour. Accepting the challenge, Clay, cutting and driving brilliantly, hit 58 in sixty-eight minutes. His stand with Poole produced 62 in half an hour. Despite the loss of wickets, Nottinghamshire never gave up the quest for runs. Although wickets were lost, Dooland, Butler and Jepson hit out lustily and the 200 was passed with 3 wickets left. Lock, ably supported by his fieldsmen, restored the balance however, and largely through his fine effort Surrey were able to gain their exciting victory. When the last over of extra time was begun either side had a chance to win the match, for Nottinghamshire, with the last pair together, wanted 7 runs for victory.

The 1955 Surrey team. From left to right, back row: H. Strudwick (scorer), B. Constable, P.J. Loader, T.H. Clark, G.A.R. Lock, E.A. Bedser, D.G.W. Fletcher, J.C. Laker, R.C.E. Pratt, J. Tait(masseur), A. Sandham (coach). Front row: M.J. Stewart, A.J.W. McIntyre, P.B.H. May, W.S. Surridge, A.V. Bedser, K.F. Barrington.

In an atmosphere of suppressed excitement Lock sent down the first ball of this vital over and Giles, acting as runner for Kelly (hurt while fielding), called Rowe for a run. Before Rowe could get to the other end, however, Subba Row had flung the ball back to McIntyre, who broke the wicket to the accompaniment of a triumphant cry from the Surrey players and spectators. In spite of this tragic ending, Nottinghamshire deserved all praise for never giving up in their run chase.

SURREY v. NOTTINGHAMSHIRE

Played at The Oval on 1st, 3rd and 4th August 1953 [3-day Match]   Toss: Not known
Surrey won by 6 runs

SURREY

D.G.W. Fletcher	c Butler b Stocks	61	c Simpson b Dooland	16
T.H. Clark	st Rowe b Stocks	35	c Simpson b Dooland	38
P.B.H. May	not out	135	not out	73
B. Constable	c Rowe b Dooland	54	c Baxter b Stocks	29
E.A. Bedser	not out	35		
R. Subba Row				
#A.J.W. McIntyre				
J.C. Laker				
*W.S. Surridge				
A.V. Bedser				
G.A.R. Lock				
Extras	b 2, lb 6	8	lb 10, w 1	11
Total	**(for 3 wickets declared)**	**328**	**(for 3 wickets declared)**	**167**

NOTTINGHAMSHIRE

*R.T. Simpson	st McIntyre b Lock	88	lbw b Lock	15
J.D. Clay	c & b Lock	89	c & b Lock	58
C.J. Poole	c Clark b Laker	2	b Lock	26
F.W. Stocks	c & b Surridge	23	st McIntyre b Laker	13
R.J. Giles	b Laker	3	lbw b Lock	17
A.G. Baxter	lbw b Laker	0	lbw b Lock	6
B. Dooland	c Lock b A.V. Bedser	1	c & b A.V. Bedser	24
J. Kelly	c & b Clark	26	[10] not out	0
H.J. Butler	lbw b Surridge	30	[8] c Clark b Lock	11
A. Jepson	not out	18	[9] c A.V. Bedser b Lock	18
#E.J. Rowe	c Lock b Surridge	0	run out	0
Extras	b 3, lb 1, nb 3	7	b 2, lb 11, nb 1	14
Total	**(all out)**	**287**	**(all out)**	**202**

Bowling

NOTTINGHAMSHIRE	O	M	R	W	O	M	R	W
Butler	24	4	56	0	10	2	29	0
Jepson	23	4	58	0	19	1	60	0
Dooland	35	9	93	1	12	2	49	2
Kelly	29	7	70	0				
Stocks	16	6	43	2	3	0	18	1

SURREY	O	M	R	W	O	M	R	W
A.V. Bedser	24	11	30	1	13	1	54	1
Surridge	26.5	8	85	3	2	0	18	0
Laker	35	12	72	3	9	0	32	1
Lock	29	7	89	2	19.1	1	84	7
Clark	5	3	4	1				

FALL OF WICKETS

	S	N	S	N
1st	75	159	29	29
2nd	126	172	95	91
3rd	246	182	167	116
4th	–	193	–	122
5th	–	193	–	143
6th	–	208	–	148
7th	–	208	–	172
8th	–	255	–	200
9th	–	272	–	202
10th	–	287	–	202

Umpires: P. Corrall and A.E. Pothecary

SURREY v. NORTHAMPTONSHIRE

Date: 4-5 August 1954   County Championship
Location: Kettering

When Surrey began their nineteenth Championship match at the end of July their prospects of becoming the first county for fifteen years to win the title three times in succession looked extremely slender. With ten matches to play they stood eighth in the table, 46 points behind Yorkshire the leaders. Even though Yorkshire had played two games more, few except the Surrey players thought much of their hopes. Nor were they playing in the manner of potential champions.

Then came a most remarkable transformation. By consistently dynamic cricket, Surrey swept aside all remaining opposition, taking 112 points from a possible 120 and finished 22 points ahead of Yorkshire, the runners-up. In that period of thorough domination, Surrey raced to five victories in two days and the only game they did not win outright was that against Middlesex at The Oval, which rain virtually turned into a one-day fixture. In a way they might be deemed fortunate that during the closing weeks of the season the weather held them up less than most counties and generally the toss favoured them, but those were minor reasons for their success. Above all, the retention of the title came about through the supremacy of the attack, supported by fielding of uncommon excellence together with the initiative and imagination of the captain, Surridge, who so accurately assessed the tactical risks and possibilities of each situation. Of few players would it be more true to say that his batting and bowling averages completely misrepresented the full value of Surridge to the side. Surridge thought and acted in terms of attack from the first ball and once again the force of his own drive infected his men.

The power of Surrey's reserve strength was adequately reflected by the second eleven winning the Minor Counties' championship, in which youth played so vital a part.

Laker was the hero of an exciting Surrey victory by 1 wicket over Northamptonshire at Kettering. After bowling splendidly in both innings for a match analysis of 11 for 94, he played a fighting innings of 33 not out to carry his side through a trying situation in the closing stages. The pitch always helped spin bowlers and on the first day 24 wickets fell for 319 runs. Chiefly through Broderick, who dismissed the last three batsmen for 1 run, Northamptonshire gained a first innings lead of 4 runs.

The game had been remarkably close and thrilling throughout. On the last day Northamptonshire lost their

Jim Laker batting.

remaining 6 second-innings wickets for 60 on a pitch further affected by rain. Tribe and Broderick offered resistance for ninety minutes in adding 50 runs for the fifth wicket. Then Laker came back to strike the vital blow by including them both in 3 wickets that he took in 11 balls for no runs.

Tyson quickly struck two blows for Northamptonshire, dismissing Stewart and May for 13. Clark's 32 and Barrington's 22, however, were valuable innings in Surrey's fightback. Laker remained master of the situation in the Northamptonshire second innings, but Surrey, set 138 to win, lost 6 wickets for 100. Almost immediately Subba Row, who had been batting confidently, fell to a smart catch by Starkie. Laker, however, drove with power and took cleverly placed and quickly run singles to retain most of the bowling. But he lost Alec Bedser at 119 and Lock at 131. For several overs Tribe and Broderick bowled too accurately for Laker to attempt the big hit he wanted. Finally it was Loader who turned Tribe to leg for 2 and the winning hit.

SURREY v. NORTHAMPTONSHIRE

Played at Kettering on 4th and 5th August 1954 [3-day Match]   Toss: Not known
Surrey won by 1 wicket

NORTHAMPTONSHIRE

*D. Brookes	c Lock b Loader	2	b Laker		10
A.P. Arnold	c Stewart b Laker	10	c Stewart b Lock		7
#L. Livingston	c Barrington b Lock	45	b Lock		27
F. Jakeman	c Subba Row b Laker	13	c Bedser b Laker		1
G.E. Tribe	c Laker b Lock	9	c Stewart b Laker		35
V. Broderick	lbw b Laker	6	b Laker		13
B.L. Reynolds	c Stewart b Laker	3	b Laker		0
F.H. Tyson	b Laker	1	c May b Bedser		4
J. Wild	b Lock	5	b Lock		11
S. Starkie	c Stewart b Laker	8	not out		1
R.W. Clarke	not out	13	lbw b Bedser		0
Extras	b 7, lb 2, nb 1	10	b 13, lb 10, nb 1		24
Total	**(all out)**	**125**	**(all out)**		**133**

SURREY

T.H. Clark	c Wild b Starkie	16	st Livingston b Tribe		32
M.J. Stewart	st Livingston b Broderick	21	b Tyson		5
*P.B.H. May	c Starkie b Broderick	2	hit wkt b Tyson		7
B. Constable	b Starkie	9	run out		12
K.F. Barrington	lbw b Broderick	17	st Livingston b Broderick		22
R. Subba Row	b Broderick	4	c Starkie b Broderick		13
#A.J.W. McIntyre	st Livingston b Tribe	22	c Wild b Tribe		6
J.C. Laker	lbw b Broderick	18	not out		33
A.V. Bedser	not out	7	c Wild b Tribe		2
G.A.R. Lock	c & b Broderick	0	lbw b Tribe		2
P.J. Loader	b Broderick	0	not out		2
Extras	b 3, lb 2	5	b 2, nb 1		3
Total	**(all out)**	**121**	**(for 9 wickets)**		**139**

Bowling

SURREY	O	M	R	W	O	M	R	W
Bedser	5	0	21	0	17.2	9	11	2
Loader	3	0	5	1				
Laker	17.5	3	58	6	21	12	36	5
Lock	16	3	31	3	29	9	62	3
Clark					2	2	0	0

NORTHAMPTONSHIRE	O	M	R	W	O	M	R	W
Tyson	3	0	11	0	6	2	14	2
Clarke	3	0	12	0				
Broderick	18.4	8	38	7	26	7	61	2
Starkie	14	1	43	2	7	2	12	0
Tribe	4	0	12	1	17.3	8	30	4
Wild					4	0	19	0

FALL OF WICKETS

	N	S	N	S
1st	3	31	17	5
2nd	59	41	39	13
3rd	63	41	43	44
4th	85	60	61	65
5th	88	70	111	83
6th	90	73	111	100
7th	93	103	114	102
8th	104	119	130	119
9th	106	119	133	131
10th	125	121	133	–

Umpires: H. Elliott and H. Elliott

SURREY v. WORCESTERSHIRE

Date: 25-26 August 1954   **County Championship**
Location: The Oval

When Worcestershire came to The Oval on 25 August 1954 Surrey needed only to win the match to retain the County Championship title for the third year in succession. Rain had affected the wicket and play could not begin until 2 p.m. Surridge won the toss and asked Worcestershire to bat. In 100 minutes they were bowled out for 25, which was the lowest score hit against Surrey in the twentieth century. The last 8 Worcestershire wickets went down for 5 runs, Lock taking 5 for 2 in 33 balls. Lock's astonishing figures speak for themselves; he was accurate and completely deadly, turning the ball venomously and occasionally making it lift as well. Laker was no less steady if a shade less hostile and Bedser played his part by getting rid of the only two formidable Worcestershire batsmen before giving way to spin. Moreover, the fielding was alert and sure as always it had been under Surridge's leadership.

Surrey's innings, coming on top of this debacle, was in sharpest contrast. May put Surrey ahead with 1 wicket down, and he immediately celebrated with a magnificent cover-drive. His driving was superb and it was altogether a little gem of an innings. Suddenly, Surridge declared and, with a possible eighty minutes left in the day, Lock and Laker, after rubbing the new ball in the mud, were again at Worcestershire's throats. Fielders swarmed round the bat and in a quarter of an hour Kenyon and Outschoorn had been caught close to the wicket. It seemed that the incredible might happen and Surrey win within an afternoon and evening. But now Richardson showed his mettle with a first-rate defensive innings and Broadbent was stubbornness itself, leaving Worcestershire at 13 for 2 when stumps were drawn.

Within an hour next morning, Surrey had won. At one time, Worcestershire were 18 for 6 and it was only a few shots by Yarnold as fielders clustered round the wicket that boosted the score to 40. It was appropriate on this of all occasions, that the quality that Surrey revealed above others was their catching near to the wicket. Laker held a blinding snick at second slip off an attempted drive by Jenkins; Bedser held another one almost as quick at first slip and McIntyre took his chances like the reliable wicketkeeper he was. Laker bowled unchanged from the Pavilion End, taking the important wicket of Richardson in his first over when the batsman tried to avoid a ball that lifted. From the Vauxhall End Bedser attacked with much hostility until the last man came in, when Loader accepted the opportunity of taking his 100th wicket of the season. He became the fourth Surrey bowler to do so, all of them cheaply, which was another indication of their strength. Having scored only 92 themselves, Surrey had won by an innings and 27 runs in little more than five hours of cricket.

Peter May driving with Godfrey Evans keeping wicket.

Peter May had fond memories of the match: 'Worcestershire were short of spin in those days, the pitch seemed easier and I was enjoying myself when to my astonishment I saw Stuart appear on the balcony and declare. Our score was 92 for 3. In those days the amateurs still used the upstairs dressing room. Downstairs among the rest of the side the general verdict was that the captain must have gone mad. His explanation as he led us out was that it was going to rain, which did not entirely clear up the misgivings.'

Most of the Surrey members and supporters were of a similar opinion, but in the event he was looked upon in awe as Surrey triumphed.

SURREY v. WORCESTERSHIRE

Played at The Oval on 25th and 26th August 1954 [3-day Match]   Toss: Surrey
Surrey won by an innings and 27 runs

WORCESTERSHIRE

D. Kenyon	c Surridge b Bedser	8	c Stewart b Lock		6
P.E. Richardson	c May b Bedser	0	c McIntyre b Laker		9
L.F. Outschoorn	b Laker	9	c Lock b Laker		3
R.G. Broadbent	c Laker b Lock	3	c McIntyre b Laker		1
N. Hughes	run out	0	hit wkt b Bedser		2
L.N. Devereux	not out	2	retired hurt		1
R.O. Jenkins	c Stewart b Lock	1	c Laker b Bedser		1
#H. Yarnold	c Barrington b Lock	1	not out		14
*R.T.D. Perks	c Barrington b Laker	0	b Bedser		2
J.A. Flavell	c Constable b Lock	0	c Clark b Laker		3
J.R. Ashman	c & b Lock	0	c Bedser b Loader		2
Extras	lb 1	1	lb 1, nb 1		2
Total	**(all out)**	**25**	**(all out)**		**40**

SURREY

T.H. Clark	c Richardson b Perks	10
M.J. Stewart	c Flavell b Perks	11
P.B.H. May	not out	31
B. Constable	c & b Ashman	29
K.F. Barrington	not out	10
#A.J.W. McIntyre		
J.C. Laker		
*W.S. Surridge		
A.V. Bedser		
G.A.R. Lock		
P.J. Loader		
Extras	w 1	1
Total	**(for 3 wickets declared)**	**92**

Bowling

SURREY	O	M	R	W	O	M	R	W
Bedser	9	4	12	3	6	3	7	3
Loader	6	3	5	0	2.4	1	3	1
Laker	8	3	5	2	17	9	25	4
Lock	5.3	4	2	5	10	7	3	1

WORCESTERSHIRE	O	M	R	W
Perks	12	1	43	2
Flavell	3	1	17	0
Ashman	8	3	29	1
Devereux	1	0	2	0

FALL OF WICKETS

	W	S	W
1st	1	12	0
2nd	16	31	5
3rd	20	77	13
4th	20	–	16
5th	21	–	16
6th	23	–	18
7th	25	–	23
8th	25	–	26
9th	25	–	40
10th	25	–	–

Umpires: F.S. Lee and E. Cooke

The aggregate of runs is the lowest for a completed match in the County Championship.

SURREY v. YORKSHIRE

Date: 4, 6-7 June 1955

County Championship

Location: The Oval

Surrey, desperately pursued by Yorkshire, won the Championship for the fourth consecutive season with Stuart Surridge as their captain, a feat only twice previously accomplished under the same leader, namely by Yorkshire, captained by A.B. Sellers from 1937 to 1946, and Nottinghamshire, by Alfred Shaw from 1883 to 1886. Again Surrey owed their success to their brilliance in the field, where Surridge once more set a wonderful example by his enthusiastic and enterprising leadership as well as his splendid catching. As many as seven Surrey players appeared for England (Yorkshire provided six) but, thanks to their capable understudies, Surrey were usually able to fill the gaps adequately, though for the most part the batting was thin in the absence of May.

The meeting of these two great rivals for the Championship drew crowds of Test match proportions on the first two days and altogether 45,000 paid, a collection for McIntyre in his benefit match yielding £535. With the ground saturated, Yardley sent in Surrey and they were all out in two-and-a-half hours, the batsmen being helpless against Appleyard, whose rising off-spinners made his leg trap a persistent danger. With Hutton bowled for a duck in his second consecutive innings, Yorkshire, for whom Watson batted admirably, took three hours to gain the lead. Every ball mattered and no one complained that six hours' cricket on the first day yielded only 193 runs. Lock bowled magnificently for Surrey and in dismissing Lowson made a marvellous right-handed return catch while lying on the pitch. The pitch was never difficult to the extent of making the game a travesty. Before lunch the occasional ball turned and lifted nastily, and the one that accounted for May did so almost unplayably. Many of the other batsmen were out to strokes of poor quality, and Watson alone remained with dignity.

Batting a second time on Monday, Surrey found that the sun of the weekend had sapped the moisture from the pitch and left it dry and easy. However, runs were at a premium and they exercised great care, Fletcher, for instance, taking four-and-a-half hours over 84. Yardley shuffled his bowlers about with almost bewildering frequency. After another excellent innings by May 5 wickets fell in the last session to bring Yorkshire back into the match, Surrey holding a lead of 215 at the close with 3 wickets in hand.

Peter Loader bowling.

As the players arrived for the last day they were greeted with heavy rain but play was resumed after an hour's delay. Surrey declared at their overnight score, leaving Yorkshire to score at 50 runs an hour to force a victory. They found themselves trapped on a difficult pitch and lost 2 wickets for 4 runs, including the valuable scalp of Hutton. Wilson was dismissed just after lunch but then Watson and Sutcliffe put together a partnership that raised the hopes of the Yorkshire supporters. At 3 p.m. Yorkshire needed 135 in 150 minutes with 7 wickets in hand. At 82 Watson was the victim of a horrible ball from Lock that turned as sharply as it lifted and finished in short leg's hands. Surrey made things much harder for themselves by missing five catches until Sutcliffe's fine effort of defensive skill lasting two hours twenty minutes was ended by Bedser sticking out a massive left hand and taking a return catch. Appleyard and Trueman held up Surrey for twenty-five minutes in a last-wicket stand but Surrey came through to victory in the end. The match provided something unique in the appearance of the two current England captains, May and Hutton, serving under their official county captains Surridge and Yardley.

SURREY v. YORKSHIRE

Played at The Oval on 4th, 6th and 7th June 1955 [3-day Match]   Toss: Yorkshire
Surrey won by 41 runs

SURREY

Batsman	Dismissal	Runs	Dismissal (2nd)	Runs
T.H. Clark	c Lowson b Trueman	7	c Booth b Trueman	33
D.G.W. Fletcher	c Sutcliffe b Appleyard	12	c Wardle b Close	84
P.B.H. May	c Trueman b Appleyard	6	c & b Trueman	56
B. Constable	c Watson b Appleyard	5	not out	32
K.F. Barrington	c Close b Appleyard	1	b Wardle	11
#A.J.W. McIntyre	c Watson b Appleyard	10	b Wardle	9
J.C. Laker	c Wilson b Appleyard	0	c sub b Close	5
*W.S. Surridge	b Trueman	10	c Appleyard b Close	15
G.A.R. Lock	not out	21	not out	0
P.J. Loader	b Wardle	5		
A.V. Bedser	c & b Appleyard	0		
Extras	b 5, lb 3	8	b 9, lb 5, nb 2	16
Total	**(all out)**	**85**	**(for 7 wickets declared)**	**261**

YORKSHIRE

Batsman	Dismissal	Runs	Dismissal (2nd)	Runs
L. Hutton	c McIntyre b Loader	0	b Loader	1
F.A. Lowson	c & b Lock	16	c Lock b Bedser	0
J.V. Wilson	c Surridge b Laker	10	c Barrington b Lock	9
W.H.H. Sutcliffe	b Lock	7	c & b Bedser	40
W. Watson	b Loader	32	c Surridge b Lock	30
D.B. Close	b Lock	1	c Barrington b Laker	3
*N.W.D. Yardley	c McIntyre b Lock	24	lbw b Bedser	15
J.H. Wardle	c Lock b Bedser	2	b Bedser	41
#R. Booth	b Loader	22	c May b Bedser	3
F.S. Trueman	b Loader	4	not out	14
R. Appleyard	not out	1	c Laker b Lock	9
Extras	b 4, lb 7, w 1	12	b 6, nb 2, w 1	9
Total	**(all out)**	**131**	**(all out)**	**174**

Bowling

YORKSHIRE	O	M	R	W	O	M	R	W
Trueman	15	2	32	2	22	7	37	2
Appleyard	18	6	29	7	30	9	66	0
Wardle	6	2	16	1	27	9	47	2
Close					29	7	87	3
Yardley					4	1	8	0

SURREY	O	M	R	W	O	M	R	W
Loader	20.3	5	38	4	12	2	38	1
Bedser	9	3	18	1	25	11	38	5
Lock	27	12	36	4	25.2	8	63	3
Laker	12	7	23	1	15	6	26	1
Surridge	2	1	4	0				

FALL OF WICKETS

	S	Y	S	Y
1st	20	0	67	2
2nd	22	28	167	4
3rd	28	30	205	32
4th	32	64	225	82
5th	39	66	235	85
6th	41	95	242	100
7th	52	99	261	133
8th	62	111	–	141
9th	74	126	–	150
10th	85	131	–	174

Umpires: D.E. Davies and T.W. Spencer

SURREY *v.* THE AUSTRALIANS

Date: 16-18 May 1956
Location: The Oval

This match went down in the record books as in the first Australian innings Jim Laker took all 10 wickets. It was the first time since 1878 that a bowler had taken all 10 Australian wickets, and even then the bowler had been a Surrey man, Edward Barratt.

Laker began at 12.20 p.m. from the Pavilion End and he continued for four hours twenty minutes, interrupted only by the lunch and tea intervals, and he bowled scarcely a loose ball. Laker came in to bowl broad of beam and red-faced, and he continued to the end, completely unemotional, ponderous, his shoulders hunched. Always he hitched his trousers before bowling, always he licked his fingers; always he forced the ball into his grip and his run up never varied, his legs hardly bending at the knees, his weight on his heels, his strides short. Lock, who was Laker's partner for 23 overs, was in comparison almost totally ineffective. He turned and flighted the ball less and he was not so accurate. He played, however, an important part, for although he conceded 100 runs he never allowed the batsmen to get on top.

It might be assumed from Laker's figures that he received a lot of help from the pitch, but this is not so. It is true that by tea-time the dust was flying but his success was his and his alone and off the other bowlers only one chance was given. Four of his wickets came with the ball that floated away to the slips, drawing the bat with it. The first wicket fell at 62. Laker had been bowling for forty minutes then and Burke was his first victim, leg-before, shouldering his bat. McDonald fought on, looking as he invariably did, an ungainly but uncompromising opponent. Mackay pushed deliberately forward for fifty minutes like a boxer jabbing at a punch bag. Four singles he acquired and nothing seemed more probable than that sooner or later Laker would find the edge of his bat. Sure enough he did so with the total at 124 and by then the crowd was dozing off in the afternoon sun, with Mackay as the sedative. Slowly, however, they came to their senses as Laker hauled in his victims and by 5 p.m. the ground was charged with excitement. From time to time perhaps Surridge thought of taking the new ball but one by one the wickets came and when Maddocks and Lindwall were out in the over after tea there was no doubt that Laker would not be robbed of fame by lack of opportunity.

Jim Laker catching John Haves of the New Zealanders off his own bowling in 1949 when Surrey played the tourists.

Harvey was caught at mid-wicket forcing off his legs, and McDonald, when he had

Above left: Bernie Constable.

Above right: Tony Lock bowling.

scored 89 in three hours thirty-five minutes, moved in to drive Laker and was caught at the third attempt by Swetman. Miller was quite unrecognisable as the cavalier stroke-maker. His first 3 runs took forty-five minutes and at tea he had made only 12 in the hour. Four hours of cricket had taken the Australians to 173 for 4, and within ten minutes of the interval Laker had struck three more quick blows without conceding another run.

Davidson threw his bat at the ball, sending Laker for one magnificent six to mid-wicket, making 21 in a quarter of an hour. Crawford did much the same, scoring 16 in three hits, including two towering sixes to long-on. But Laker always had the last word, and finally he was left with Miller or Wilson to complete his collection. Cox dropped Miller off Lock at 217 and for twenty-five minutes Wilson did, with great coolness, what Miller asked of him. After much tension a tired Laker had Wilson caught at the wicket and everyone was happy.

In the evening when Fletcher and Clark made 34 confident runs in the last thirty-five minutes the Australians were quick to turn to spin. Crawford bowled only 1 over before Johnson rubbed the ball in the dust to remove its shine and trod through Laker's well-worn footfalls. At the other end Davidson soon replaced Lindwall but neither imparted such spin as Laker.

The point of the Australian strategy on the second day eluded most people and could have convinced no one. Surrey had looked the better side throughout but it must be many a day since a team from Australia

Surrey v. The Australians

played so poorly without character or phlegm. The fast bowlers, Lindwall and Crawford, kept their sweaters on all day although both were perfectly fit and the new ball was available at 3 p.m. Moreover, Constable was notoriously uncertain against speed, and the slow bowlers were unable to extract any venom from the pitch. Johnson bowled for five-and-a-quarter hours with only one short break of twenty-five minutes. Generally speaking he was comfortably played, for he hardly turned a ball. Fletcher and Clark found the set-up to their liking, dealing Johnson some juicy blows off the front foot. Both were in form and they showed Surrey the way to set about things, a lead that was admirably followed until May was out ten minutes after lunch. Clark was caught at the wicket reaching out at Burke and May was beaten in the air by Johnson and stumped on the leg side. Between lunch and tea 80 runs came from the bat, 54 of them from Constable. After tea Laker, with some robust driving, stormed to 43 in thirty-nine minutes. The crowd enjoyed Laker's batting almost as much as they had his bowling, for with a burst of 16 he put Surrey ahead and when he was gone Surridge took over the assault. It was now that Constable, after four-and-a-half hours, reached his painstaking, well-earned century. Soon afterwards he was caught and bowled trying to hit Johnson back over his head and the innings lingered on until 6.10 p.m. Surrey's last 4 wickets had added 126 in ninety-five minutes.

On the third day Surrey became the first English county for forty-four years to lower the colours of an Australian team. However, over the years, Surrey have beaten the Australians 9 times in 48 matches. This time it was Lock who put the Australians to rout and at one stage there was a chance that Lock would emulate Laker's first-innings achievement. The most significant moment of the day came at 11.45 a.m. Laker had begun from the Pavilion End and Lock from the Vauxhall End, but McDonald and Burke had batted cautiously and without undue trouble. The bowlers changed ends and Lock saw his first ball rear angrily at Burke. McDonald and Burke had to be prised out and all credit to them for that. The rest variously spent a few desperate moments at the crease, baffled beyond hope by Lock and palpably without any answer to his spin. The four fielders at slip or gully took three catches, Swetman one and the short legs the others. The last 9 wickets fell in sixty-five minutes, while just 34 runs were being scored, hardly one of them off the middle of the bat. Surrey were left just 20 runs to win, which they accomplished without losing a wicket.

This match had a strong bearing on the Test match series, which England went on to win. Laker took 46 wickets in the Test series, including 19 at Old Trafford, a world record that has never been equalled, let alone beaten.

SURREY _v._ THE AUSTRALIANS

Played at The Oval on 16th, 17th and 18th May 1956 [3-day Match]   Toss: The Australians
Surrey won by 10 wickets

THE AUSTRALIANS

J.W. Burke	lbw b Laker	28	c & b Lock		20
C.C. McDonald	c Swetman b Laker	89	c Laker b Lock		45
K.D. Mackay	c Surridge b Laker	4	lbw b Laker		4
R.N. Harvey	c Constable b Laker	13	c May b Lock		10
K.R. Miller	not out	57	c Swetman b Lock		2
#L.V. Maddocks	b Laker	12	c Laker b Lock		0
R.R. Lindwall	b Laker	0	c Constable b Lock		4
*I.W.G. Johnson	c Swetman b Laker	0	run out		5
A.K. Davidson	c May b Laker	21	c May b Laker		7
W.P.A. Crawford	b Laker	16	not out		5
J.W. Wilson	c Swetman b Laker	4	st Swetman b Lock		1
Extras	b 4, lb 8, nb 3	15	lb 4		4
Total	**(all out)**	**259**	**(all out)**		**107**

SURREY

D.G.W. Fletcher	c Maddocks b Johnson	29	not out		9
T.H. Clark	c Maddocks b Burke	58	not out		8
B. Constable	c & b Johnson	109			
P.B.H. May	st Maddocks b Johnson	27			
K.F. Barrington	c Miller b Johnson	4			
#R. Swetman	st Maddocks b Davidson	0			
D.F. Cox	b Davidson	13			
J.C. Laker	c McDonald b Johnson	43			
*W.S. Surridge	c Harvey b Johnson	38			
G.A.R. Lock	b Davidson	0			
P.J. Loader	not out	12			
Extras	b10, lb 3, w 1	14	b1, lb 1, nb 1		3
Total	**(all out)**	**347**	**(for no wicket)**		**20**

Bowling

SURREY	O	M	R	W	O	M	R	W
Loader	15	4	30	0	2	2	0	0
Surridge	8	2	8	0	1	1	0	0
Laker	46	18	88	10	25	10	42	2
Lock	33	12	100	0	31.1	9	49	7
Cox	5	0	18	0				
Clark					8	4	12	0

AUSTRALIANS	O	M	R	W	O	M	R	W
Lindwall	2	1	10	0	8	4	8	0
Crawford	1	0	4	0	7	3	9	0
Johnson	60.3	12	168	6				
Davidson	44	14	101	3				
Wilson	19	9	34	0				
Burke	7	2	16	1				

FALL OF WICKETS

	A	S	A	S
1st	62	53	56	–
2nd	93	112	73	–
3rd	124	147	83	–
4th	151	192	85	–
5th	173	195	85	–
6th	173	221	89	–
7th	175	278	92	–
8th	199	302	101	–
9th	217	313	104	–
10th	259	347	107	–

Umpires: L.H. Gray and K.H. McCanlis

Surrey v. Kent

Date: 7, 9-10 July 1956   **County Championship**
Location: Blackheath

In the Kent second innings at Blackheath Tony Lock took all 10 wickets for 54 runs and his figures for the match were 16 for 83. To this day the figures remain a record for the County and a personal record for Lock. It gave proof that his worries during the previous fortnight, suspected appendicitis and a broken toe, had in no way lessened his ability.

Kent were completely outplayed in a match notable chiefly for Lock's bowling and the batting of Clark and May. In excellent conditions, Tom Clark batted masterfully on the first day, hitting the biggest score of his career. Peter May, who helped to add 174 in two hours, batted far more convincingly than when scoring a century against Kent a week earlier, much of his stroke-play being superb.

Weekend rain added to Kent's plight. On the Monday, when Surridge declared at the start of play, Lock received enough help from the turf to shatter Kent's moderate batting. Turning the ball from the start, slowly in the beginning, he was helped by some poor batting, only Cowdrey showing any fighting spirit in Kent's first innings, and there were many fine strokes in his 49. Cowdrey's departure at 91 was the beginning of a collapse in which 6 wickets fell while 10 runs were scored. Apart from Cowdrey only Phebey, to a lesser extent, could counter Lock's biting leg-spin and when Kent followed on even these two succumbed quickly. By the close Lock was in sight of all 10 wickets for the first time and this he achieved the following morning by dismissing the last four batsmen without conceding a run. His total match haul made his figures for the two games against Kent in 1956 26 wickets for 143 runs.

Tony Lock came through the Surrey Colts system to make his debut for the first team just eight days after his seventeenth birthday in 1946. In his career for the county he took 1,713 wickets until 1963, after which he emigrated with his family to Australia where he played for Western Australia. He was one of the greatest fielders in the game, usually positioned at short leg. During his 385 matches for the County he took 533 catches.

Surrey, enthusiastically led by Stuart Surridge, carried off the Championship for the fifth consecutive year, an achievement without parallel. There was no doubt that once again Surrey were the best-equipped side in the Championship. During their five triumphant years under Surridge they were, perhaps, fortunate in being able to call on the same nucleus of players. Looking at the names of the men who took Surrey to the top in 1952, one finds that the only two notable personalities who left their ranks were Laurie Fishlock and Jack Parker.

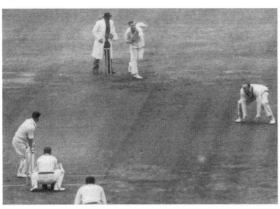

Tony Lock bowling against Worcestershire in 1949.

In 1956 Surrey were always in a challenging position, but they did not head the Championship table until the first week of July and then their tenure was insecure, for Lancashire mostly led the way in June and July. Subsequently, four successive wins against Essex, Middlesex (twice) and Sussex in August carried Surrey ahead and they had to be thankful that they had some games in hand for, owing to the weather, none of the last five Championship matches produced a definite result.

SURREY *v.* KENT

Played at Blackheath on 7th, 9th and 10th July 1956 [3-day Match]   Toss: Surrey
Surrey won by an innings and 173 runs

SURREY

T.H. Clark	b Ridgway	191
M.J. Stewart	c Fagg b Wright	13
K.F. Barrington	c Ridgway b Wright	32
P.B.H. May	not out	128
R.E.C. Pratt	c Phebey b Page	21
E.A. Bedser	not out	11
#R. Swetman		
*W.S. Surridge		
G.A.R. Lock		
A.V. Bedser		
P.J. Loader		
Extras	lb 8	8
Total	**(4 wickets declared)**	**404**

KENT

A.H. Phebey	b Lock	22	b Lock		12
M.C. Cowdrey	c Swetman b A.V. Bedser	49	lbw b Lock		8
R.C. Wilson	c Barrington b Lock	2	b Lock		32
T.G. Evans	b Loader	1	c & b Lock		19
A.E. Fagg	c Stewart b Lock	2	c A.V. Bedser b Lock		21
A.L. Dixon	c May b Lock	13	b Lock		2
#D.G. Ufton	b Lock	0	not out		17
F. Ridgway	c Surridge b Lock	6	c Stewart b Lock		7
D.J. Halfyard	c Pratt b A.V. Bedser	1	c Barrington b Lock		0
J.C.T. Page	not out	1	b Lock		0
*D.V.P. Wright	c Loader b A.V. Bedser	2	b Lock		0
Extras	lb 2	2	b 6, lb 5, nb 1		12
Total	**(all out)**	**101**	**(all out)**		**130**

Bowling

KENT	O	M	R	W
Ridgway	15	3	53	1
Halfyard	28	4	104	0
Wright	25	3	85	2
Page	25	2	107	1
Dixon	9	0	44	0
Cowdrey	1	0	3	0

SURREY	O	M	R	W	O	M	R	W
Loader	16	6	38	1	8	3	7	0
A.V. Bedser	11	0	28	3	16	5	41	0
Lock	21	12	29	6	29.1	18	54	10
E.A. Bedser	3	2	4	0	18	10	16	0

FALL OF WICKETS

	S	K	K
1st	47	55	20
2nd	145	63	29
3rd	319	64	60
4th	360	67	84
5th	—	91	101
6th	—	91	104
7th	—	91	130
8th	—	96	130
9th	—	98	130
10th	—	101	130

Umpires: H. Elliott and W.F.F. Price

SURREY v. YORKSHIRE

Date: 21, 23-24 July 1956   **County Championship**
Location: Bramall Lane, Sheffield

Surrey won by 14 runs and completed their first double over Yorkshire for thirty-six years. In their first innings, Surrey, sent in to bat, began well, Stewart and Barrington putting on 73 for the second wicket. The fourth wicket fell at 103 and then came complete collapse, the last 6 going down in forty minutes for 25. Illingworth took 3 wickets in 4 balls during one over.

By the end of the second day's play Yorkshire were left in a commanding position, and certainly a great deal better placed than seemed probable after the first half-hour, when the score stood at 104 for 7. Alec Bedser and Loader bowled unchanged during the morning, while Yorkshire took their score to 189, due largely to a masterful innings by Close. In this crisis for Yorkshire Close took command, attacking from the start. In one expensive over from Alec Bedser Close drove him twice beautifully through the covers, but eventually ran out of partners.

Surrey started their second innings disastrously. May came in just before 1 p.m. as both Clark and Stewart had been dismissed with only 5 runs on the board. Peter May was his usual confident self and, after lunch, the score rose to 99 before Barrington was caught at the wicket. May moved to his fifty with grace and elegance before falling to a mistimed drive off Illingworth. After brief resistance from Eric Bedser and McIntyre the innings closed at 6 p.m., leaving Yorkshire needing just 97 for victory. Loader struck back immediately, seeing Lowson and Wison back in the pavilion with only 2 runs on the board before the close of play.

There had been showers overnight, but the pitch was unaffected and, like the clock, it was on the side of the batsmen. Yorkshiremen will try to forget quickly the humiliating performance that their county put up, but for many the image of the pitiful and hesitant groping for the 67 runs required for victory while 8 wickets remained will fade slowly and not without anguish.

The task seemed easy, but it was at once apparent that neither batsman was happy against Loader and Alec Bedser. Watson fell leg before to Bedser and Taylor was then dismissed in the same manner by Loader, having batted an hour-and-a-half for his 13 runs. Sutcliffe stayed for an hour but the collapse began with Taylor's departure. Lock bowled Close and had Sutcliffe caught by May. Illingworth stayed for half an hour but was then caught and bowled by Lock. The score was 56 for 7 and Trueman joined Wardle. Ignoring the advice of a well-wisher in the crowd, Wardle decided that anything was better than defence and, following his natural bent, attacked from the start. He drove Loader for six into the pavilion, took four through the slips and turned Lock to leg for another boundary. Lock then had him caught and bowled and Trueman, Broughton and Binks added only 7 between them.

Lock took 5 of the last 6 wickets, and in his 11 overs had 7 maidens and only 11 runs were scored off him, while Loader managed 8 wickets for 115 runs. Yorkshire lost 8 wickets for 52 runs on a wicket that contained no unfriendliness and certainly no spite.

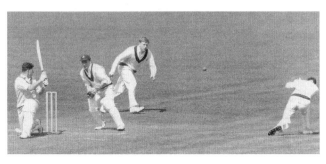

Ken Barrington batting against Lancashire.

SURREY *v.* YORKSHIRE

Played at Bramall Lane, Sheffield on 21st, 23rd and 24th July 1956 [3-day Match]   Toss: Yorkshire
Surrey won by 14 runs

SURREY

T.H. Clark	lbw b Broughton	5	c Watson b Broughton		0
M.J. Stewart	run out	42	b Broughton		1
K.F. Barrington	b Broughton	34	c Binks b Wardle		35
P.B.H. May	b Illingworth	16	c Trueman b Illingworth		68
B. Constable	run out	6	c & b Trueman		4
E.A. Bedser	b Wardle	8	c Close b Illingworth		26
#A.J.W. McIntyre	b Illingworth	0	c & b Wardle		11
*W.S. Surridge	lbw b Illingworth	0	c Sutcliffe b Wardle		7
G.A.R. Lock	c & b Wardle	7	b Wardle		5
A.V. Bedser	c Close b Illingworth	5	b Illingworth		0
P.J. Loader	not out	3	not out		0
Extras	b 2	2			0
Total	**(all out)**	**128**	**(all out)**		**157**

YORKSHIRE

F.A. Lowson	lbw b Loader	1	b Loader		2
K. Taylor	b E.A. Bedser	8	lbw b Loader		13
J.V. Wilson	c May b A.V. Bedser	62	b Loader		0
W. Watson	b Loader	14	lbw b A.V. Bedser		23
*W.H.H. Sutcliffe	b Lock	0	c May b Lock		5
#J.G. Binks	b A.V. Bedser	0	b Loader		4
D.B. Close	not out	58	b Lock		5
R. Illingworth	c Lock b A.V. Bedser	0	c & b Lock		3
J.H. Wardle	c Clark b Loader	18	c & b Lock		18
F.S. Trueman	b A.V. Bedser	15	b Lock		3
P.N. Broughton	lbw b Loader	0	not out		0
Extras	b 7, lb 6	13	b 4, lb 2		6
Total	**(all out)**	**189**	**(all out)**		**82**

Bowling

YORKSHIRE	O	M	R	W	O	M	R	W
Trueman	15	4	31	0	15	4	29	1
Broughton	13	3	24	2	8	3	20	2
Wardle	26	13	30	2	29	12	62	4
Illingworth	22.3	4	38	4	22.3	7	34	3
Close	2	1	3	0	1	0	5	0
Taylor					7	3	7	0

SURREY	O	M	R	W	O	M	R	W
Loader	28.4	7	75	4	22.1	9	40	4
A.V. Bedser	24	9	56	4	17	9	25	1
Lock	14	3	39	1	11	7	11	5
E.A. Bedser	7	3	6	1	3	3	0	0

FALL OF WICKETS

	S	Y	S	Y
1st	35	2	0	2
2nd	78	28	5	2
3rd	92	75	99	40
4th	103	78	104	44
5th	113	83	113	51
6th	113	104	137	52
7th	113	104	149	56
8th	117	151	157	75
9th	124	188	157	82
10th	128	189	157	82

Umpires: L.H. Gray and T.W. Spencer

Surrey v. Northamptonshire

Date: 5-7 June 1957

Location: Northampton

County Championship

On the first day the first 3 Northamptonshire wickets fell for only 9 runs, and the last 5 for 68. Fortunately Barrick propped up the middle with a splendid innings lasting over three hours, so that the home side escaped an ignominious total. The wicket, greener than usual at Northampton, gave Alec Bedser in particular a certain amount of help. Yet Barrick and Lightfoot at once settled down to watchful batting and restored a sense of proportion. By the afternoon the wicket was playing more easily and if Laker had not been to hand to tantalize both batsmen with his varied flight Northamptonshire might even have gained control of the situation. Laker, whose first 41 deliveries were not scored off, gradually forced Lightfoot onto the back foot and then beat him, the fourth wicket having added 77 in 105 minutes. Tribe then added 59 with Barrick for the fifth wicket and immediately after the tea interval Barrick's admirable innings came to an end.

Tactically, the second day showed honours to be more or less even. By mid-afternoon, when May and Barrington were in possession and Surrey within 50 of the Northamptonshire total with only 3 wickets down, Brookes set a defensive field to which Allen in particular bowled splendidly. It was a measure of his success that May took three-and-a-quarter hours to make 96 out of 146. Barrington was at the crease seventy-five minutes for 10; Eric Bedser was restrained to 5 in his first hour but McIntyre's aggressive designs paid handsome dividends. Northamptonshire were generally efficient in the field with some brilliant efforts by Allen and Manning, and Allen bowled to a fine length for some seventy-five minutes before tea, when his 14 overs had cost only 22 runs. True, he came in for punishment late in the day, but this was only when the batsmen were willing to chance their arm. Surrey eventually finished the day with a first-innings lead of 98.

The last day saw Micky Stewart establish a new record for first-class cricket by taking seven catches in Northamptonshire's second innings. No fielder in first-class cricket other than a wicketkeeper had previously taken so many during a single innings, and only twice had even a wicketkeeper held seven. On rain-affected turf, Stewart fielded very close to the accurate bowling of Alec Bedser, Lock and Laker, taking six catches at backward short leg and one in the gully. None was really difficult, yet he earned great credit for the clean manner in which he took everything that came his way at such close range. He ended the season by taking 77 catches and in his career a total of 605, both Surrey records.

Surrey went on to win this match by ten wickets and won the County Championship for the sixth year in a row by a record margin. They went to the head of the table on 11 June and claimed the title on 16 August. In their most successful season under the captaincy of Peter May they won 21 of their 28 championship matches, 9 of them inside two days. Second in the table were Northamptonshire, some 94 points behind having won 15 matches. As Peter May was also captain of England, he insisted on having an official vice-captain. Alec Bedser filled this role to perfection, working closely throughout with his captain.

Micky Stewart at full stretch in the field.

SURREY v. NORTHAMPTONSHIRE

Played at Northampton on 5th, 6th and 7th June 1957 [3-day Match]   Toss: Not known
Surrey won by 10 wickets

NORTHAMPTONSHIRE

*D. Brookes	c Lock b A.V. Bedser	7	c Lock b A.V. Bedser	6
B.L. Reynolds	b Loader	2	c Stewart b A.V. Bedser	26
L. Livingston	b A.V. Bedser	0	c Stewart b A.V. Bedser	0
D.W. Barrick	c McIntyre b Lock	86	c Barrington b A.V. Bedser	33
A. Lightfoot	lbw b Laker	29	c Stewart b Lock	5
G.E. Tribe	b E.A. Bedser	22	c Stewart b Lock	11
J.S. Manning	b E.A. Bedser	0	c Stewart b Laker	10
#K.V. Andrew	run out	6	not out	12
F.H. Tyson	not out	34	c Stewart b Laker	4
M.H.J. Allen	b A.V. Bedser	5	c McIntyre b Lock	0
H.R.A. Kelleher	b Laker	13	c Stewart b Lock	0
Extras	b 2, lb 6, nb 1	9	b 4	4
Total	**(all out)**	**213**	**(all out)**	**111**

SURREY

D.G.W. Fletcher	c Manning b Tribe	37	not out	8
M.J. Stewart	c Andrew b Manning	24	not out	6
B. Constable	b Allen	42		
*P.B.H. May	c Kelleher b Tyson	96		
K.F. Barrington	b Kelleher	10		
E.A. Bedser	c Livingston b Tyson	46		
#A.J.W. McIntyre	b Tribe	27		
G.A.R. Lock	st Andrew b Tribe	0		
J.C. Laker	c Manning b Tribe	11		
P.J. Loader	c Brookes b Tribe	4		
A.V. Bedser	not out	0		
Extras	b 7, lb 7	14		0
Total	**(all out)**	**311**	**(for no wicket)**	**14**

Bowling

SURREY	O	M	R	W	O	M	R	W
Loader	26	9	54	1	9	2	26	0
A.V. Bedser	26	6	58	3	16	5	43	4
Laker	13.3	10	14	2	12	6	14	2
Lock	23	10	45	1	9.2	1	20	4
E.A. Bedser	16	2	33	2	1	0	4	0

NORTHAMPTONSHIRE	O	M	R	W	O	M	R	W
Tyson	25.4	8	47	2				
Kelleher	22	7	39	1				
Manning	26	10	81	1	1.5	1	8	0
Tribe	26	3	73	5				
Allen	20	8	57	1	1	0	6	0

FALL OF WICKETS

	N	S	N	S
1st	9	58	11	–
2nd	9	78	11	–
3rd	9	157	52	–
4th	86	212	59	–
5th	145	224	71	–
6th	145	269	87	–
7th	147	281	95	–
8th	161	299	98	–
9th	184	310	101	–
10th	213	311	111	–

Umpires: F.S. Lee and A. Skelding

SURREY v. WORCESTERSHIRE

Date: 23, 25-26 August 1958   **County Championship**
Location: Worcester

Surrey won this match by 9 wickets, taking all 14 points. Though being without May, Laker and Lock because of Test calls, Surrey were always the masters. Runs did not come easily, however, on a soft turf but missed catches gave lives to Fletcher, Constable and Barrington, otherwise their first innings total would have been considerably less than 270. How little Worcestershire could afford such errors was emphasised on the second day, when they were caught on a drying pitch. Alec Bedser, leading Surrey in the absence of Peter May, found conditions to his taste. On turf that was recovering from the previous week's storms he contrived all sorts of problems for the Worcestershire batsmen. He began by taking a wicket with the first ball of the day, which Outschoorn chopped into his stumps, and when Worcestershire's first innings ended at 82 Bedser had a fine analysis of 6 for 25. He consistently moved the ball a little either way off the seam, and to add to the batsmen's difficulties he made it swing in the heavy atmosphere. In spite of the poverty of the Worcestershire scorecard, Bedser and Gibson, who gave his captain useful support, could seldom make the ball hit more than stump high. Worcestershire offered stiffer resistance when they followed on 188 runs behind, Dews and Slade combining in an excellent stand of 46 runs. With these two parted through a spectacular one-handed catch by McIntyre, the end was in sight and Surrey won with more than two hours to spare.

The invincible march of Surrey continued in 1958. During their next match they became County Champions for the seventh year in succession, and it was difficult to foresee the most redoubtable force of the future emulating, let alone surpassing, Surrey's record, which has no parallel in English cricket.

Their latest triumph was not all plain sailing. Illness, injury and heavy representative calls presented many difficulties and they needed all their high skill, resource, team spirit and determination to preserve their standing. On the eve of the season Alec Bedser, the vice-captain, went down with pneumonia and his exceptional bowling power and tactical guidance was lost until 4 July when he played in his first Championship fixture. Even after that date he was not able to play regularly. In one of the worst seasons for weather in memory Surrey warded off a determined challenge from Hampshire. They won only 14 matches but this was two more than Hampshire and Somerset, who finished third.

The season could be divided into three sharply defined phases. Their first five championship matches brought handsome victories, three by an innings. Then followed a bleak mid-season spell with defeats at the hands of Somerset and Yorkshire, and the loss of first-innings points to Hampshire, their most dangerous rivals. But in the last vital weeks Surrey recaptured their old form and vitality. Middlesex were twice defeated, and an important week fell during the Fifth Test. Despite a weakened side Surrey collected valuable points from Northamptonshire and Worcestershire in this match. In the absence of May and Bedser the captaincy was taken over by McIntyre, who was in his last season before becoming the county's coach. Fortunately for Surrey, McIntyre not only kept wicket with his usual efficiency (many thought he would have been a wise choice for the tour to Australia in 1958/59) but made many useful scores with the bat. He was not found wanting as a leader.

David Gibson.

SURREY *v.* WORCESTERSHIRE

Played at Worcester on 23rd, 25th and 26th August 1958 [3-day Match]　　　　　Toss: Not known
Surrey won by 9 wickets

SURREY

T.H. Clark	b Flavell	14	c Broadbent b Flavell		24
A.B.D. Parsons	c Dews b Aldridge	0	not out		14
D.G.W. Fletcher	lbw b Flavell	78	not out		10
M.J. Stewart	c Booth b Slade	54			
B. Constable	b Pearson	57			
K.F. Barrington	c Richardson b Pearson	28			
E.A. Bedser	c Horton b Aldridge	15			
#A.J.W. McIntyre	b Aldridge	1			
D. Gibson	b Aldridge	0			
*A.V. Bedser	not out	8			
P.J. Loader					
Extras	b 5, lb 5, nb 5	15	b 1, lb 2		3
Total	**(for 9 wickets declared)**	**270**	**(for 1 wicket)**		**51**

WORCESTERSHIRE

*D. Kenyon	b Loader	2	c McIntyre b Gibson		31
L.F. Outschoorn	b A.V. Bedser	4	c McIntyre b Loader		30
M.J. Horton	c Stewart b A.V. Bedser	25	c McIntyre b Loader		23
D.W. Richardson	run out	20	b Gibson		26
R.G. Broadbent	b Gibson	10	lbw b E.A. Bedser		17
G. Dews	lbw b Gibson	2	b E.A. Bedser		53
#R. Booth	c Barrington b A.V. Bedser	1	b Gibson		7
D.N.F. Slade	not out	10	c McIntyre b Loader		29
D.B. Pearson	b A.V. Bedser	0	lbw b E.A. Bedser		6
K.J. Aldridge	lbw b A.V. Bedser	2	c Stewart b E.A. Bedser		0
J.A. Flavell	b A.V. Bedser	6	not out		1
Extras		0	b 4, lb 3, nb 5		12
Total	**(all out)**	**82**	**(all out)**		**235**

Bowling

WORCESTERSHIRE	O	M	R	W	O	M	R	W
Flavell	24	10	51	2	7	1	16	1
Aldridge	21.3	4	69	4	4	0	19	0
Slade	26	11	49	1				
Pearson	24	5	58	2	2	0	8	0
Horton	11	3	28	0				
Kenyon					0.4	0	5	0

SURREY	O	M	R	W	O	M	R	W
Loader	14	4	42	1	25	4	78	3
A.V. Bedser	17.2	8	25	6	25	10	59	0
Gibson	9	3	15	2	24	6	56	3
E.A. Bedser					27.4	13	29	4
Barrington					1	0	1	0

FALL OF WICKETS

	S	W	W	S
1st	8	6	51	38
2nd	23	6	85	–
3rd	109	39	92	–
4th	190	57	134	–
5th	233	59	139	–
6th	252	64	155	–
7th	253	64	201	–
8th	253	64	230	–
9th	270	70	230	–
10th	–	82	235	–

Umpires: W.E. Phillipson and A.E. Pothecary

Surrey v. Essex

Date: 4, 6-7 July 1959

County Championship

Location: The Oval

On winning the toss, Surrey made a good start with Micky Stewart (one six, sixteen fours) and Fletcher, who, driving and hooking skilfully, put on 171 in three hours ten minutes. Unfortunately, the rest of the side made little contribution as the total rose to an eventual 312. On the second day Essex lost three men in their first innings for 47, Taylor being out to a typical falling catch by Stewart in the gully. Only the batting of Insole and Bailey threatened Surrey's lead but after adding 90 Insole was caught at the wicket off Bedser and the rest of the innings disintegrated, the last 6 wickets falling for 29. When Surrey batted again 146 ahead, John Edrich, lbw to the first ball on the opening day, hit his seventh century of the season that earned him his county cap. He and Fletcher shared an unfinished partnership of 136 as Bedser declared the innings closed.

Needing 342 to win at 67 an hour, Essex always struggled and, despite a plucky innings lasting three-and-a-quarter hours by Insole, suffered defeat in the seventh minute of extra time. Barker and Savill began by adding 41 in under an hour before Lock surprised Barker with a faster one. At 66 Savill was caught at forward short leg off bat and pad, and just before lunch Taylor, after some crisp strokes, hooked Laker to mid-on. Essex, never primarily concerned with going for the runs, began the afternoon with Insole and Bailey together, and they lost at the last because Insole ran out of partners. At 2.40 p.m. Bailey was caught at short leg pushing forward to an off-break that turned, and half an hour later Bear was taken at the wicket as he thrust out at Lock. With 5 wickets down and two hours twenty minutes left Surrey seemed likely to win at their ease, until Smith remained with Insole for eighty minutes.

The pitch, which was too slow to be of use to the bowlers, meant Surrey began to run short of time. Although the first 5 wickets had fallen to the spinners, Bedser must have been glad of the new ball when he claimed it with eighty minutes of play left. Loader and Gibson had first use of it but Bedser brought himself on after twenty minutes and caught Smith off his own bowling. Knight lasted a further

twenty minutes before Loader bowled him, Greensmith went the same way two balls later and Ralph was quickly trapped by Lock. Within 2 overs Surrey had virtually won the match and then Insole was caught down the leg side hooking at a short one from Loader. Victory had been achieved in the nick of time.

Earlier in the season John Edrich achieved the remarkable performance of hitting a century in each innings in only his second Championship match against Nottinghamshire at Trent Bridge. In the whole season he scored 1,799 runs at 52.91 and in his very successful career made 103 centuries and played for England in 77 Test matches. He was captain of the county from 1973 to 1977.

Yorkshire ended Surrey's reign of seven years as champions after one of the most thrilling fights for a long time. The closing phases of the competition were most exciting, with Yorkshire, Gloucestershire, Surrey and Warwickshire all in with a chance. It seemed that Surrey would again be champions until they failed to take a point from their last two matches.

John Edrich.

SURREY v. ESSEX

Played at The Oval on 4th, 6th and 7th July 1959 [3-day Match] Toss: Surrey
Surrey won by 136 runs

SURREY

J.H. Edrich	lbw b Bailey	0	not out		103
M.J. Stewart	c Clarke b Ralph	140	c Smith b Clarke		36
D.G.W. Fletcher	lbw b Ralph	89	not out		40
T.H. Clark	lbw b Clarke	13			
B. Constable	c Taylor b Clarke	8			
D. Gibson	c & b Bailey	11			
G.A.R. Lock	c Bear b Knight	23			
#A.J. McIntyre	c Savill b Clarke	13			
J.C. Laker	not out	10			
P.J. Loader	c Insole b Clarke	1			
*A.V. Bedser	b Insole	1			
Extras	lb 3	3	b 8, lb 8		16
Total	**(all out)**	**312**	**(for 1 wicket declared)**		**195**

ESSEX

G. Barker	b Gibson	10	b Lock		23
L.A. Savill	c McIntyre b Gibson	21	c Lock b Laker		26
#B. Taylor	c Stewart b Bedser	0	c Loader b Laker		23
*D.J. Insole	c McIntyre b Bedser	62	c McIntyre b Loader		65
T.E. Bailey	c McIntyre b Lock	53	c Stewart b Laker		7
M. Bear	c Lock b Bedser	8	c McIntyre b Lock		8
G.J. Smith	lbw b Lock	0	c & b Bedser		0
B.R. Knight	c Bedser b Gibson	0	b Loader		13
W.T. Greensmith	c Bedser b Lock	0	b Loader		0
L.H.R. Ralph	c Laker b Lock	9	c Bedser b Lock		0
Dr C.B. Clarke	not out	0	not out		0
Extras	lb 2, w 1	3	b 5, nb 2		7
Total	**(all out)**	**166**	**(all out)**		**205**

Bowling

ESSEX	O	M	R	W	O	M	R	W
Bailey	23	2	74	2	12	3	31	0
Ralph	25	3	62	2	12	1	33	0
Knight	16	1	51	1	11	2	32	0
Clarke	19	4	56	4	13	1	49	1
Insole	10.3	1	24	1	2	0	12	0
Greensmith	10	1	42	0	6	0	22	0

SURREY	O	M	R	W	O	M	R	W
Loader	13	3	22	0	13.2	2	34	3
A.V. Bedser	17	5	42	3	16	3	38	1
Gibson	13.1	2	27	3	14	4	36	0
Laker	9	0	23	0	17	3	33	3
Lock	17	5	49	4	28	4	57	3

FALL OF WICKETS

	S	E	S	E
1st	0	16	59	41
2nd	171	21	–	66
3rd	210	47	–	77
4th	224	137	–	100
5th	249	155	–	112
6th	269	157	–	178
7th	300	157	–	198
8th	300	157	–	198
9th	302	166	–	198
10th	312	166	–	205

Umpires: J.H. Parks and John Langridge

Surrey v. Derbyshire

Date: 1-3 September 1971   **County Championship**
Location: The Oval

Storey, with an admirable century that retrieved Surrey's bad start to the match, and Intikhab, taking 9 wickets in the match with his leg-breaks, took the main credit for a win that put Surrey well within striking distance of the Championship. In the absence of Edrich with back trouble, Surrey collapsed against the opening attack of Ward and Buxton, but Storey, finding a partner in Lewis in a sixth-wicket stand of 103, brought about a recovery. Lewis had been brought up from Mitcham, where he was to have played for the second eleven, to replace Edrich and played a valuable part in Surrey's recovery. By the time Lewis arrived on the ground Long, who went in with Stewart, had been leg-before, and soon afterwards Roope, aiming to clear the short-leg boundary, skied Buxton to the wicketkeeper. Younis played with due responsibility for seventy minutes before Ward had him caught at slip, and Owen-Thomas did the same until he was bowled by Ward. Their first 43 overs yielded 85 runs, and even Storey was having a struggle to get going. For him the fight began to show in a couple of overs from Russell and Buxton, in which he hit three cracking fours and a six into the forecourt of the public house by the gasometer. With Lewis joining in with a hook and a drive for four off Ward, 32 runs came off 5 overs and Surrey's problems eased. Both Lewis and Intikhab were run out but Storey went on to reach his hundred.

On the second day Stewart declared when Storey was dismissed for 164, the best score of his career. It was a terribly slow pitch and for a side such as Derbyshire, whose main concern was survival, the slowness of the pitch was no great irritation. The leg breaks of Intikhab turned, albeit gently, and with 3 wickets in forty minutes before tea he enabled Surrey to make slightly more progress than had begun to seem likely. In mid-afternoon Long was hit on the cheek by a ball from Pocock that lifted a little and brushed Page's pad. Long went off to be stitched up, leaving Roope to keep wicket, and he accepted the second stumping chance that Page allowed him. Hall batted three hours ten minutes for his 95 before being caught by Arnold on the square-leg boundary. Harvey made 18 in seventy minutes at a time when Derbyshire should have been accelerating.

On the third day Stewart left Derbyshire to make 205 to win in 165 minutes. It was a sensibly tempting declaration, and without being reckless Derbyshire never lost sight of the target. Willis, bowling very fast, took 2 wickets in his second over. Then Wilkins and Russell led a run-chase, but Intikhab took the last 5 wickets and Surrey won with ten minutes to spare. Surrey had won because they had a leg spinner to tickle out the tail.

Surrey, at the last gasp, won the County Championship for the eighteenth time outright and for the first time since 1958. Yet the final triumph bore an unsatisfactory and discordant note as, on a sunny day at Southampton in mid-September, they just managed a second bowling bonus point in Hampshire's first innings to draw level with Warwickshire and take the title on the basis of more wins, 11 to 9, though well beaten in the last match.

Stuart Storey.

SURREY *v.* DERBYSHIRE

Played at The Oval on 1st, 2nd and 3rd September 1971 [3-day Match]   Toss: Surrey
Surrey won by 40 runs

SURREY

*M.J. Stewart	c Ward b Buxton	6	c Ward b Swarbrook		16
#A. Long	lbw b Ward	1	not out		11
G.R.J. Roope	c Taylor b Buxton	5	run out		3
Younis Ahmed	c Wilkins b Ward	23	st Taylor b Russell		40
D.R. Owen-Thomas	b Ward	22	c Swarbrook b Russell		1
S.J. Storey	c Harvey b Swarbrook	164	c Page b Russell		41
R.M. Lewis	run out	35	run out		26
Intikhab Alam	run out	11	run out		0
P.I. Pocock	c Buxton b Ward	4	c Hall b Russell		38
R.G.D. Willis	not out	29			
G.G. Arnold					
Extras	lb 5, w 1, nb 9	15	b 1, lb 9, nb 1		11
Total	**(for 9 wickets declared)**	**315**	**(for 8 wickets declared)**		**187**

DERBYSHIRE

P.J.K. Gibbs	b Pocock	11	b Willis		1
I.W. Hall	c Arnold b Intikhab	95	b Pocock		16
M.H. Page	st Roope b Intikhab	28	b Willis		0
C.P. Wilkins	c Owen-Thomas b Intikhab	10	c Long b Pocock		43
J.F. Harvey	b Willis	18	b Intikhab		16
*I.R. Buxton	not out	79	st Long b Pocock		6
#R.W. Taylor	st Long b Intikhab	21	hit wkt b Intikhab		24
P.E. Russell	c Long b Storey	24	not out		41
F.W. Swarbrook	not out	0	c Stewart b Intikhab		4
E. Smith			lbw b Intikhab		5
A. Ward			c Willis b Intikhab		0
Extras	b 6, lb 3, nb 3	12	b 3, lb 5		8
Total	**(for 7 wickets declared)**	**298**	**(all out)**		**164**

Bowling

DERBYSHIRE	O	M	R	W	O	M	R	W
Ward	29	7	74	4	13	2	45	0
Buxton	24	9	61	2	2	1	7	0
Wilkins	5	0	20	0				
Smith	11	3	29	0	1	0	13	0
Russell	13	4	39	0	17.1	5	60	4
Swarbrook	21.2	6	77	1	10	1	51	1

SURREY	O	M	R	W	O	M	R	W
Arnold	17	3	44	0	5	3	6	0
Willis	15	3	34	1	5	0	23	2
Intikhab	33	6	87	4	21.2	1	63	5
Pocock	24	6	68	1	18	1	54	3
Storey	6	0	20	1	4	1	10	0
Roope	7	0	33	0				

FALL OF WICKETS

	S	D	S	D
1st	2	28	25	2
2nd	12	127	45	2
3rd	23	143	48	60
4th	54	157	128	65
5th	70	201	135	81
6th	173	254	135	91
7th	213	292	139	134
8th	226	–	187	150
9th	315	–	–	162
10th	–	–	–	164

Umpires: J. Arnold and A.E. Fagg

SURREY v. SUSSEX

Date: 12, 14-15 August 1972   **County Championship**
Location: Eastbourne

This was one of those games where most of the excitement was crammed into the last quarter of an hour, when the batsmen were reduced to gibbering wrecks and somehow the bowlers got out of jail after the key had seemed to be firmly lodged in the jailer's pocket. Correction, not bowlers – bowler. Pat Pocock chose this match to turn in one of the most remarkable spells of bowling. He took 7 wickets in 11 balls as Sussex blew the simple task of getting 18 off the last 3 overs with 9 wickets in hand.

Until 6 p.m. on the third day, the match had followed a fairly routine pattern, even if some good cricket had been played. Both sides made up for the loss of almost all the first day's play with some positive batting on the second day, Monday. After putting on 130 for Surrey's first wicket, Mike Edwards and Roy Lewis both got out, mistiming their shots in the quest for bonus points. In the last hour of the day, the spin and guile of Pocock and Intikhab troubled Sussex and they were indebted to a fine unbeaten half-century from Roger Prideaux. Given a couple of sensible declarations on the final day, there was every prospect of a good finish.

Prideaux got his hundred, then, after Sussex declared behind, Surrey took up the challenge and made some quick runs before Micky Stewart declared for the second time. Sussex were asked to get 205 in seventy minutes plus 20 overs. By 6 p.m. it was all over bar the final rituals. Prideaux and Greenidge had added 160 in eighty minutes and at 187 for 1, Sussex were nearly home. With 9 wickets in hand all they had to do was to push the ball around for ones or twos with just one boundary needed.

Pat Pocock began the eighteenth of the last 20 overs and with the first ball bowled Greenidge. Mike Buss suffered the same fate third ball. Jim Parks got two runs off the fourth ball, failed to score off the fifth and was caught and bowled from the sixth. At least Sussex would now have to work for the last 16 in 2 overs. Jackman, bowling the penultimate over, conceded 11 runs, including a six over long-on by Mike Griffith. Sussex needed another 5 runs with 6 wickets in hand and Prideaux must have fancied a

Pat Pocock spinning away.

hundred in each innings as one good blow would also finish the match. Off Pocock's first ball, Prideaux went for it, but he top-edged a sweep and Jackman caught him near the boundary. The batsmen crossed while the ball was in the air and Griffith holed out in 'cowshot corner' going for the clinching blow. Jerry Morley came in with Pocock on a hat-trick. As the batsmen charged down the pitch Pocock bowled a quicker one and Arnold Long was left to complete a routine stumping. Although the ball hit Long's pads and rebounded half a yard away the keeper managed to complete the dismissal.

It was now 200 for 7 with 3 balls left. John Spencer got a single off the fourth ball, so just one slog would do it. Tony Buss went for it but was bowled, heaving across the line. Joshi aimed a desperate heave at the last ball but could score only one, being run out attempting an impossible second run. The last over had yielded 5 wickets, 2 runs and a hat-trick. It had taken ten minutes to bowl the final over and Pat Pocock had taken 7 wickets for 4 runs in his last 2 overs. He has been dining out on these incredible figures ever since.

SURREY *v.* SUSSEX

Played at Eastbourne on 12th, 14th and 15th August 1972 [3-day Match]   Toss: Surrey
Match drawn

SURREY

*M.J. Stewart	not out	34	not out		1
R.M. Lewis	c Greenidge b M.A.Buss	72	st Parks b Spencer		28
D.R. Owen-Thomas	c Parks b Spencer	31	c Griffith b M.A. Buss		32
Younis Ahmed	c Parks b Phillipson	26	c A. Buss b Joshi		26
G.R.J. Roope	not out	43	not out		21
M.J. Edwards	c Joshi b M.A. Buss	81	c Phillipson b Spencer		6
Intikhab Alam			c Spencer b Joshi		6
A.R. Butcher					
#A. Long					
P.I. Pocock					
R.D. Jackman					
Extras	b 6, lb 7	13	b 4, lb 6		10
Total	**(for 4 wickets declared)**	**300**	**(for 5 wickets declared)**		**130**

SUSSEX

G.A. Greenidge	c Long b Butcher	6	b Pocock		68
P.J. Graves	b Pocock	35	c Roope b Jackman		14
R.M. Prideaux	not out	106	c Jackman b Pocock		97
M.A. Buss	c Long b Pocock	8	b Pocock		0
#J.M. Parks	c Roope b Intikhab	29	c & b Pocock		2
*M.G. Griffith	not out	29	c Lewis b Pocock		6
J. Spencer	lbw b Intikhab	0	not out		1
J.D. Morley			st Long b Pocock		0
A. Buss			b Pocock		0
U.C. Joshi			run out		1
C.P. Phillipson					
Extras	b 6, lb 7	13	b 4, lb 8, w 1		13
Total	**(for 5 wickets declared)**	**226**	**(for 9 wickets)**		**202**

Bowling

SUSSEX	O	M	R	W	O	M	R	W
Spencer	22.5	4	56	1	11	0	29	2
A. Buss	17	3	74	0	12	1	35	0
Phillipson	13	1	37	1				
M.A. Buss	15	3	58	2	5	1	29	1
Joshi	15	5	62	0	6	0	27	2

SURREY	O	M	R	W	O	M	R	W
Jackman	7	1	29	0	13	1	62	1
Butcher	15	4	33	1	3	0	13	0
Pocock	24	8	69	2	16	1	67	7
Intikhab	26.1	6	82	2	12	2	47	0

FALL OF WICKETS

	Sur	Sus	Sur	Sus
1st	130	12	8	27
2nd	167	80	61	187
3rd	212	104	95	187
4th	232	117	101	189
5th	–	190	117	200
6th	–	–	–	200
7th	–	–	–	200
8th	–	–	–	201
9th	–	–	–	202
10th	–	–	–	–

Umpires: D.J. Constant and A.G.T. Whitehead

Surrey v. Middlesex

Date: 1-3 July 1987   **County Championship**

Location: The Oval

Over 1,200 runs in the match showed the batting strength of both sides. The bowlers worked admirably throughout the game, but without luck. On the first day play was dour until the fifty-fifth over. In the end Middlesex were comfortably placed thanks to a solid 60 by Keith Brown, 74 from Roland Butcher and an undefeated century from Downton. During the afternoon Keith Medlycott kept Middlesex shackled to a run rate little above 2 runs an over. Shackled, that is, until Butcher found himself at peace with the world. He reached his fifty off 77 balls, and so large was he seeing the ball that in one hectic spell of 16 balls he plundered 30 runs. Paul Downton, nourished but not misled by this display, moved sedately on.

It was obvious during the second day that due to the slowness of the pitch it would need enterprising declarations from the captains to force a result. Middlesex declared overnight and Surrey started with a century partnership. Graeme Clinton's 93 assured Surrey of a useful total and bore such an air of permanence that his demise was the day's major surprise. Darren Bicknell, his partner, played with more freedom after surviving a chance to short leg off the third ball of the day from Daniel and, next ball, finding himself at the same end as Clinton but scrambling to safety by the grace of Slack's misfield. Thereafter, Surrey progressed thoughtfully until a slog foreshadowed the declaration. Andy Needham and Phil Tufnell sent down 67 of Middlesex's 104 overs on a hot day. Tufnell, with two fine catches to supplement his 3 wickets, had a hand in every Surrey wicket until Hughes also contributed by bowling a line and length with the old ball and removed Clinton.

The final day saw Surrey being set 334 runs to win from 62 overs. Middlesex, in the shape of Wilf Slack and John Carr, had resumed with 54 on the board and an overall lead of 115. Without undue haste, the opening pair swept the score along at more than 4 runs an over. Slack was the senior partner and, after he had been caught at close mid-on, Carr and Brown continued to flourish, Carr moving to and past his hundred with a series of graceful strokes.

Downton's declaration never appeared to err on the side of generosity. When Simon Hughes removed Clinton with a beauty, Darren Bicknell followed with only 15 on the board and Lynch's timing appeared to have deserted him forever, there were gloomy faces among the Surrey members. As Monte Lynch found his feet and Stewart moved serenely on, the fielding became ragged in the heat of the day and it was the supporters of Middlesex who reached for a restorative drink.

Alec Stewart scored as fine a hundred as one would like to see. He made 127 from 159 balls and with

Alec Stewart batting against Warwickshire in 2003.
(Empics)

Lynch (95) put on 208 in 42 overs. That Surrey won off the last ball, having continued the chase as wickets tumbled, will not have come amiss either. Surrey needed 41 off 4 overs, and then 11 off the last, with Tony Gray and Martin Bicknell at the wicket. The first 4 balls yielded 4 runs and Bicknell it was who faced Needham with 7 required from the last 2 balls. A skimming six over long off brought the scores level and then a scampered single saw Surrey home to their second successive championship win.

SURREY v. MIDDLESEX

Played at The Oval on 1st, 2nd and 3rd July 1987 [3-day Match]   Toss: Middlesex
Surrey won by 2 wickets

MIDDLESEX

Batsman	Dismissal	Runs	Dismissal	Runs
W.N. Slack	b Gray	0	c Greig b Medlycott	96
J.D. Carr	c Greig b Gray	20	not out	123
K.R. Brown	c Brown b Thomas	60	not out	42
C.T. Radley	lbw b Thomas	26		
R.O. Butcher	c Stewart b Greig	74		
*#P.R. Downton	not out	103		
A. Needham	lbw b Thomas	0		
S.P. Hughes	c Greig b MP Bicknell	15		
A.R.C. Fraser	lbw b MP Bicknell	0		
W.W. Daniel	not out	3		
P.C.R. Tufnell				
Extras	b 11, lb 7, w 1, nb 17	36	b 3, lb 4, w 1, nb 3	11
Total	**(for 8 wickets declared)**	**337**	**(for 1 wicket declared)**	**272**

SURREY

Batsman	Dismissal	Runs	Dismissal	Runs
D.J. Bicknell	c Slack b Tufnell	61	c Downton b Daniel	5
G.S. Clinton	c Tufnell b Hughes	93	b Hughes	0
A.J. Stewart	not out	67	b Needham	127
M.A. Lynch	c Downton b Tufnell	15	c Downton b Fraser	95
T.E. Jesty	c Downton b Tufnell	15	c Brown b Needham	29
*I.A. Greig	c Tufnell b Needham	4	c Butcher b Needham	17
D.J. Thomas	not out	8	c Butcher b Needham	6
K.T. Medlycott			run out	9
A.H. Gray			not out	9
M.P. Bicknell			not out	12
#G.E. Brown				
Extras	b 3, lb 3, w 2, nb 5	13	b 9, lb 12, w 2, nb 2	25
Total	**(for 5 wickets declared)**	**276**	**(for 8 wickets)**	**334**

Bowling

SURREY	O	M	R	W	O	M	R	W
Gray	16	2	61	2	4	0	12	0
Thomas	23	4	54	3	13	2	63	0
M.P. Bicknell	24	6	63	2	12	2	44	0
Greig	12	4	20	1	9	2	29	0
Medlycott	35	4	121	0	18.4	0	84	1
Lynch					8	0	33	0

MIDDLESEX	O	M	R	W	O	M	R	W
Daniel	6	0	20	0	17	3	71	1
Hughes	15	3	51	1	7	0	36	1
Fraser	16	4	46	0	5	0	37	1
Needham	34	9	68	1	18	0	96	4
Tufnell	33	7	85	3	15	2	73	0

FALL OF WICKETS

	M	S	M	S
1st	0	120	173	5
2nd	35	195	–	15
3rd	110	229	–	223
4th	133	247	–	261
5th	229	254	–	286
6th	236	–	–	290
7th	321	–	–	306
8th	321	–	–	319
9th	–	–	–	–
10th	–	–	–	–

Umpires: R.A. White and P.B. Wight

Surrey v. Derbyshire

Date: 12-14, 16 May 1994

County Championship

Location: The Fosters Oval

Surrey won the toss and asked their visitors to bat. Martin Bicknell and Joey Benjamin worked their way through the Derbyshire batting, each taking 4 wickets. On the second day David Ward batted stupendously. According to Mike Brearley, Ian Botham brought the spirit of the village green to Test match cricket. It is a bit crude to mark Ward down as a turbo-charged club player, but there was something bucolic about his batting. As good as a batsman as Graham Thorpe, who started friskily, was comprehensively upstaged during their third-wicket partnership of 301.

When his eye is in, few men strike the ball more cleanly than Ward, or as far. Stroke after stroke revealed his blacksmith's power after he came in at 10 for 2 and instantly took the bowlers on. In the afternoon session of the second day, with booming drives amid the lengthening shadows of toiling men, he made 105 out of 172. When Thorpe reached a creditable century of his own after tea, Ward was within 29 runs of his third double-hundred of his career, which duly arrived from 255 balls off one of his favourite strokes, the on-drive. By the close of play he had reached 216 with Surrey at 373 for 5.

As everyone knows, The Oval is not a postage-stamp ground. Undaunted by fielders at long-on and long off, Ward lifted sixes over both within the space of 3 balls from Sladdin. It was another miserable day for Sladdin who missed Thorpe, then 18, in the most inexcusable way at mid-off. Harris, a twenty-year-old medium pacer, took a wicket with his second ball in first-class cricket. Not just any old wicket but Stewart, who padded up to a ball that swung back in to him. He would have had Thorpe too, but for the mishap by Sladdin. Eventually he got his man when Thorpe swung a long hop to mid-on.

The third day was restricted due to rain and Ward extended his score to 294 in a sixth-wicket partnership of 163 with Alistair Brown who scored 92. Martin Bicknell then engineered the breakthrough by taking 2 early wickets in Derbyshire's second innings. Only one man in the Derbyshire side went down with honour. Chris Adams made a lacerating, unbeaten hundred at better than a run a ball. What better way to go to a century than by driving the bowler over his head for six? That is how he treated the ninety-fifth ball he received from Kendrick, and for good measure he struck the next ball straighter and fuller. In all, 92 of his 109 runs came

David Ward batting during his prolific season. *(Empics)*

from boundaries, his four sixes including a remarkable top-edged hook off a disgusted Bicknell. Furthermore, he was carrying a thigh strain that prevented him from coming in until the fall of the seventh wicket.

On an excellent batting pitch Derbyshire lost 15 wickets before they equalled the 294 unbeaten runs David Ward had made. Had Stewart suspected that Derbyshire's second innings would be as feeble as their first, he could well have batted on a little longer to let Ward complete Surrey's first triple-century since Jack Hobbs made one at Lord's in 1926. Surrey still wait for a modern player to reach the magic 300 figure.

David Ward was a most engaging and popular player at The Oval and his most productive season was in 1990, when he scored 2,072 runs at an average of 76.74 for Surrey including seven centuries. Following his retirement from the first-class game he became the master in charge of cricket at Whitgift School and was the moving force in Surrey now playing regularly at Croydon.

SURREY v. DERBYSHIRE

Played at The Foster's Oval on 12th, 13th, 14th and 16th May 1994 [4-day Match]   Toss: Surrey
Surrey won by an innings and 138 runs

DERBYSHIRE

P.D. Bowler	c Ward b M.P. Bicknell	15	lbw b M.P. Bicknell		5
A.S. Rollins	c Sargeant b Benjamin	10	c M.P. Bicknell b Cuffy		24
C.J. Adams	c Sargeant b M.P. Bicknell	13	[7] not out		109
*M. Azharuddin	c sub b M.P. Bicknell	34	c Ward b Benjamin		23
T.J.G. O'Gorman	c Kendrick b Benjamin	44	[3] lbw b M.P. Bicknell		2
C.M. Wells	b Kendrick	11	[5] c Sargeant b Cuffy		20
#K.M. Krikken	b Cuffy	13	[6] run out		0
A.E. Warner	c Sargeant b M.P. Bicknell	20	c Sargeant b Cuffy		7
R.W. Sladdin	lbw b Benjamin	8	c M.P. Bicknell b Benjamin		14
A.J. Harris	c Sargeant b Benjamin	10	lbw b Kendrick		1
D.E. Malcolm	not out	0	b Benjamin		10
Extras	lb 10, nb 20	30	lb 1, nb 8		9
Total	**(all out)**	**208**	**(all out)**		**224**

SURREY

D.J. Bicknell	lbw b Warner	2
*A.J. Stewart	lbw b Harris	0
G.P. Thorpe	c sub b Harris	114
D.M. Ward	not out	294
A.J. Hollioake	c Bowler b Sladdin	18
#N.F. Sargeant	c Azharuddin b Sladdin	0
A.D. Brown	lbw b Warner	92
M.P. Bicknell	not out	10
N.M. Kendrick		
J.E. Benjamin		
C.E. Cuffy		
Extras	b 1, lb 7, w 4, nb 28	40
Total	**(for 6 wickets declared)**	**570**

Bowling

SURREY	O	M	R	W	O	M	R	W
Cuffy	18.3	4	77	1	16	5	53	3
M.P. Bicknell	21	7	56	4	13	3	49	2
Benjamin	23	7	56	4	12.4	3	37	3
Kendrick	9	5	9	1	14	1	65	1
Hollioake					6	0	19	0

DERBYSHIRE	O	M	R	W
Warner	25	2	85	2
Harris	20	0	125	2
Wells	17	0	73	0
Sladdin	50	8	155	2
Adams	12	1	61	0
Azharuddin	8	0	46	0
Bowler	1	0	17	0

FALL OF WICKETS

	D	S	D
1st	21	3	5
2nd	36	10	7
3rd	43	311	49
4th	103	362	74
5th	130	364	74
6th	146	527	98
7th	177	–	124
8th	192	–	161
9th	208	–	201
10th	208	–	224

Umpires: B. Dudleston and J.H. Harris

Surrey v. Gloucestershire

Date: 26-28, 30 May 1994   **County Championship**

Location: Gloucester

After heavy rain on the first day play did not start until 1.30 p.m. on the second day of four. Gloucestershire gave a debut to Cunliffe, who had to contend with the ball darting around at the start of the innings and soon lost his wicket to Cuffy. Broad had a job to force the ball off the square and was then caught at third slip by Kendrick. Only Hancock and Wright prospered. Hancock scored 75 in a little under three hours.

Because of many interruptions for rain there were three declarations in the match. Gloucestershire terminated their first innings with 7 wickets down but Alec Stewart declared at 72 for 3, setting a challenge to the home side. They responded with a quick run chase.

On the final day it left Surrey in the position of scoring 354 from 90 overs for victory. During the final hour it looked as though it would be beyond them. Given that Courtney Walsh chose to bowl the final over, from which 8 were needed, this was perhaps the least likely of several possible results. However, Joey Benjamin swung him for four, ran for two leg byes and, although he was out to the penultimate ball, Cameron Cuffy and Mark Butcher were too quick even for Jack Russell.

Darren Bicknell was the batsman who did much to bring this about. Although he made runs for England 'A' at the start of the season he was not in the form of the previous year. A goodly number of his runs came through the 'V' between mid-off and mid-on, but his great strength lay in his timing when the quicker bowlers strayed onto his legs. He liked to pace himself and it was never possible that Surrey were likely to win. Between lunch and tea Bicknell made only 31 and yet, other than being badly missed at extra cover when on 51, was not the slightest bit ruffled.

Walsh, with his greater pace and ability, and Cooper were able to keep the run gathering within bounds. But so long as Bicknell was partnered by one of Surrey's more forceful batsmen, this scarcely mattered, although Alec Stewart made only 44 out of a first-wicket partnership of 121 that came at 4 an over. This included the shot of the day: Stewart took a stride down the pitch and dispatched a delivery thrown up by Ball to the long-off boundary.

When Stewart was leg-before to Smith, Surrey did not repine. There was Graham Thorpe to come, followed by David Ward, Alistair Brown and Adam Hollioake, with the odd slogger if required. Surrey's middle order had batted with exemplary selflessness in all competitions during the season. Here, though, they contributed all too little. Thorpe's dismissal was through an extraordinary misjudgement. He must have been five yards short of his ground when Cunliffe threw down his stumps from sideways on.

Ward was beautifully taken at second slip off Walsh and Brown was bowled by one Cooper cut back at him. Then Bicknell, having struck twenty fours, played too soon at Cooper. From the last 10 overs 59 were needed and Mark Butcher, who finished with 43, saw them through.

Through victories such as this are championships won. By the late afternoon Surrey's leadership of the table remained intact when their tenth-wicket pair scrambled a bye off the last ball for victory. However this proved to be a false dawn as they scored only seven wins in the season and finished in sixth position.

Darren Bicknell batting in 1994.
(Empics)

SURREY *v.* GLOUCESTERSHIRE

Played at Archdeacons Meadow, Gloucester on 26th, 27th, 28th and 30th May 1994 [4-day Match]
Toss: Gloucestershire
Surrey won by 1 wicket

GLOUCESTERSHIRE

B.C. Broad	c Kendrick b Butcher	24	c Brown b Cuffy	0
R.J. Cunliffe	c Sargeant b Cuffy	2	c Sargeant b Cuffy	7
T.H.C. Hancock	b Benjamin	75	c Sargeant b Cuffy	2
M.W. Alleyne	lbw b Benjamin	2	c sub b Kendrick	38
A.J. Wright	c Brown b Benjamin	87	not out	35
R.I. Dawson	c Kendrick b Cuffy	55	not out	19
#R.C. Russell	c Bicknell b Benjamin	16		
M.C.J. Ball	not out	27		
*C.A. Walsh				
A.M. Smith				
K.E. Cooper				
Extras	b 2, lb 1, w 4, nb 24	31	lb 3, nb 2	5
Total	**(for 7 wickets declared)**	**319**	**(for 4 wickets declared)**	**106**

SURREY

D.J. Bicknell	c Russell b Cooper	11	c Wright b Cooper	129
M.A. Butcher	run out	22	[7] not out	43
A.J. Hollioake	c Ball b Cooper	0	[6] c Russell b Walsh	26
G.P. Thorpe	retired hurt	28	[3] run out	6
#N.F. Sargeant	not out	5	[9] lbw b Ball	15
N.M. Kendrick	not out	0	[8] c Wright b Cooper	15
*A.J. Stewart			[2] lbw b Smith	44
D.M. Ward			[4] c Wright b Walsh	10
A.D. Brown			[5] b Cooper	5
J.E. Benjamin			c Russell b Walsh	5
C.E. Cuffy			not out	0
Extras	lb 2, nb 4	6	b 2, lb 9, w 3, nb 42	56
Total	**(for 3 wickets declared)**	**72**	**(for 9 wickets)**	**354**

Bowling

SURREY	O	M	R	W	O	M	R	W
Cuffy	29	8	80	2	8.3	1	16	3
Benjamin	31.3	10	51	4	6	2	9	0
Butcher	22	5	96	1	4	1	9	0
Kendrick	27	6	63	0	10	1	30	1
Hollioake	9	2	26	0	11	3	37	0
Stewart					1	0	2	0

GLOUCESTERSHIRE	O	M	R	W	O	M	R	W
Walsh	7	1	36	0	27	4	83	3
Cooper	9	2	24	2	25	3	99	3
Smith	8	6	2	0	17	3	80	1
Ball	5.1	3	4	0	5	0	30	1
Alleyne	1	0	4	0	16	3	51	0

FALL OF WICKETS

	G	S	G	S
1st	7	19	0	121
2nd	53	19	2	133
3rd	61	64	21	152
4th	147	–	72	157
5th	272	–	–	226
6th	278	–	–	282
7th	319	–	–	312
8th	–	–	–	340
9th	–	–	–	353
10th	–	–	–	–

Umpires: R. Julian and K.E. Palmer

SURREY v. GLOUCESTERSHIRE

Date: 27-30 April 1995   **County Championship**

Location: The Fosters Oval

Surrey feared the worst when Gloucestershire won the toss at The Oval in perfect batting conditions, having heard that Waqar Younis would not be fit to play for them in 1995. It was embarrassing enough when Monte Lynch, released the previous year after seventeen years at The Oval, was treating his old colleagues with something close to contempt, but it was downright humiliating when Andrew Symonds, only nineteen and making his championship debut, was helping himself to 161 not out from 140 balls with four sixes and twenty-one fours. Joey Benjamin took 4 wickets, including a spell of 3 for 12, which at one stage reduced Gloucestershire to 184 for 6. He had struck in the first over, claiming Wright leg-before, but Lynch gave the visitors a flying start with 46 off 58 balls, stroking eight fours in an effortless way. Then Dawson made a polished half-century.

The second day saw a feeble batting performance from Surrey in their first innings. There was no excuse for the pitiful collapse that saw them lose their last 8 wickets for 66 after Darren Bicknell and Mark Butcher had shared an opening stand of 92. Javagal Srinath, the Indian fast bowler, soon surprised Butcher with his pace and the openers could afford no liberties. They struggled along at only 2 runs per over until Bicknell, driving at a wideish ball from Alleyne, edged to gully. Srinath then produced his best spell of bowling to Alec Stewart, who managed only two singles in half an hour before he was leg-before playing back. Cooper dismissed Brown and Butcher in successive overs and, with Surrey's lengthy tail exposed, Smith finished the innings with 3 wickets for 4 runs in 17 balls. It was the first time Surrey had been forced to follow on against Gloucestershire since 1933. More teams have won after being forced to follow on at The Oval than on any other ground, but Surrey had never done it in the County Championship.

Surrey owed their victory chance to Alistair Brown. In Surrey's second innings he scored 187, beating his previous high score of 175, batting for 375 minutes and facing 297 balls.

Gloucestershire were set to score 301 to win in 86 overs, a target well within their range if they could have batted as they did in their first innings, but out of the question once they had collapsed to 44 for 5. There had been no dramatic change in the batting conditions, but Surrey's bowling was considerably better than it had been on the first day, and Gloucestershire's batting considerably worse.

Kenlock played his part by having Hodgson caught behind and bowling Wright, but it was Benjamin who undermined Gloucestershire with a sharp reminder of the whole-hearted fast-medium bowling that won him selection for England. He began by uprooting Lynch's off stump, much to the delight of his

Joey Benjamin bowling at full pace.

teammates. Two balls later he claimed Dawson leg-before, and then showed that Symonds may still have a bit to learn by tucking him up with a shortish ball that had him caught by Shahid at short leg.

Alleyne was batting well, however, and with Russell joining him in a stand of 69 in 20 overs, Surrey were beginning to fret. Spin came to the rescue in the form of Nowell, the left-arm bowler making his championship debut, and Shahid, the leg spinner recently recruited from Essex. Shahid bowled Alleyne behind his legs with his second ball, Nowell had Russell stumped after 164 minutes' resistance, and though Smith held them up for more than 9 overs in company with the defiant Ball, Benjamin completed the job when he had Smith, Gloucestershire's last man, caught at the wicket with 7 overs of this topsy-turvy match remaining.

SURREY *v.* GLOUCESTERSHIRE

Played at The Foster's Oval on 27th, 28th, 29th and 30th April, 1995 [4-day Match]   Toss: Gloucestershire
Surrey won by 93 runs

GLOUCESTERSHIRE

A.J. Wright	lbw b Benjamin	0	b Kenlock		27
G.D. Hodgson	c Nadeem Shahid b Kenlock	22	c Kersey b Kenlock		1
M.A. Lynch	c Kenlock b Hollioake	46	b Benjamin		4
R.I. Dawson	hit wkt b Benjamin	51	lbw b Benjamin		0
M.W. Alleyne	c Stewart b Benjamin	32	b Nadeem Shahid		60
A. Symonds	not out	161	c Nadeem Shahid b Benjamin		1
*#R.C. Russell	lbw b Benjamin	1	st Kersey b Nowell		56
J. Srinath	run out	16	c Butcher b Nadeem Shahid		7
M.C.J. Ball	b Hollioake	18	not out		37
K.E. Cooper	b Kenlock	32	c D.J. Bicknell b Nowell		0
A.M. Smith	c Butcher b Nowell	0	c Kersey b Benjamin		2
Extras	lb 7, nb 6	13	b 2, lb 1, w 1, nb 8		12
Total	**(all out)**	**392**	**(all out)**		**207**

SURREY

D.J. Bicknell	c Wright b Alleyne	42	lbw b Smith		45
M.A. Butcher	c Russell b Cooper	71	c Russell b Srinath		51
*A.J. Stewart	lbw b Srinath	2	c Cooper b Ball		65
A.D. Brown	c Hodgson b Cooper	16	c Lynch b Smith		187
A.J. Hollioake	lbw b Smith	27	c Lynch b Smith		32
Nadeem Shahid	run out	6	lbw b Ball		11
#G.J. Kersey	c Russell b Srinath	12	c Russell b Srinath		13
M.P. Bicknell	c Russell b Smith	9	lbw b Srinath		17
R.W. Nowell	c Russell b Srinath	0	run out		0
S.G. Kenlock	not out	4	not out		9
J.E. Benjamin	lbw b Smith	0	c Alleyne b Srinath		2
Extras	b 1, lb 7, nb 20	28	b 1, lb 9, w 2, nb 18		30
Total	**(all out)**	**217**	**(all out)**		**475**

Bowling

SURREY	O	M	R	W	O	M	R	W
M.P. Bicknell	6.3	3	17	0				
Benjamin	24	5	77	4	24	8	68	4
Kenlock	26	3	105	2	19	2	71	2
Hollioake	19.3	2	84	2	9	2	11	0
Nowell	19	5	73	1	20	11	24	2
Nadeem Shahid	5	0	29	0	7	0	30	2

GLOUCESTERSHIRE	O	M	R	W	O	M	R	W
Srinath	26	5	83	3	33.3	4	137	4
Smith	26.4	11	60	3	31	6	90	3
Ball	5	1	9	0	42	6	128	2
Cooper	20	7	22	2	24	4	65	0
Alleyne	13	4	35	1	13	2	42	0
Lynch					2	0	3	0

FALL OF WICKETS

	G	S	G	S
1st	1	96	16	96
2nd	69	103	21	124
3rd	85	151	21	223
4th	157	153	43	292
5th	166	160	44	339
6th	184	196	107	374
7th	278	202	117	414
8th	318	205	186	464
9th	371	217	186	464
10th	392	217	207	475

Umpires: J.C. Balderstone and B.J. Meyer

SURREY v. YORKSHIRE

Date: 10-12, 14 August 1995   **County Championship**
Location: The Fosters Oval

What a game. Surrey batted first and posted a 400-plus total, with Nadeem Shahid scoring 139 and Kersey a career-best 83. Nadeem Shahid had joined Surrey from Essex and in his first season for them scored 900 runs with two centuries. The 83 of Graham Kersey was to remain his best ever score as he was tragically killed in a car crash in early 1997.

Yorkshire responded with a first innings of 366, thanks mainly to a not-out innings of 153 from their most successful overseas recruit to date, the left-handed Australian, Michael Bevan. With a lead of 43, Surrey batted poorly in the second innings, the only batsmen making any significant contribution being Mark Butcher and Adam Hollioake. Silverwood took 5 wickets for the first time in his career. However, an inspired team performance in the field, led by Adam Hollioake's 4 for 22, saw Surrey victorious by 1 run. Yorkshire could blame only themselves for not securing the victory that would have moved them into fifth place behind Lancashire. Needing 219 to win, they were 185 for 3 shortly after lunch, with Moxon and Bevan batting steadily. Within the next 19 overs, they shed 7 wickets for 32 runs. When credit has duly been given to Surrey, who never gave up hope, it was a lamentable performance.

Bevan's dismissal, caught low at mid-on the ball after he had slapped Nowell over the leg boundary, did not appear threatening at the time. Moxon was there, pushing towards his hundred, and there were still 6 wickets in hand, Moxon, alas, carved Nowell to point on 90 when he could have taken four runs almost anywhere between mid-off and third man and Kellett followed at once, leg-before to Rackemann, who bowled a sturdy spell from the pavilion end.

This was a situation that needed an old head and Blakey did not provide it. His was the most culpable stroke, if stroke it can be called. He poked at a ball from Rackemann and Kersey held the catch that convinced Surrey they could yet prevail. It was the shot of a nervous beginner, not an experienced county batsman and, more than any other, it cost Yorkshire the match. For a while, Hamilton and Silverwood played sensibly, nudging 18 runs to carry Yorkshire to 215 for 7. Just 3 more were needed. Surely they could not lose.

Adam Hollioake, the Surrey captain, took the bold decision to bring himself on in Nowell's stead and he was rewarded immediately. Silverwood clipped his first ball to square leg and the very next ball Stemp slogged brainlessly to extra cover, where Shahid could hardly believe his luck. What a wicket. It was a disgracefully inappropriate stroke. Robinson survived the hat-trick ball. The conclusion was bizarre as well as desperate. Off the last ball of the next over Hollioake rapped Robinson on the pad and appealed for lbw, while the ball carried on to be well taken by Butcher at slip. Robinson indicated he had got some bat on it and the bowler was turned down, only for Butcher to appeal successfully for the catch. This lead to some remarkable scenes of celebration by the Surrey fielders.

Nadeem Shahid batting against Sussex in 2002. *(Empics)*

SURREY v. YORKSHIRE

Played at The Foster's Oval on 10th, 11th, 12th and 14th August 1995 [4-day Match]   Toss: Surrey
Surrey won by 1 run

SURREY

D.J. Bicknell	c Blakey b Hamilton	0	c Blakey b Silverwood		5
M.A. Butcher	lbw b Stemp	57	c Blakey b Stemp		62
Nadeem Shahid	lbw b Stemp	139	c Moxon b Milburn		15
A.D. Brown	b Milburn	48	b Silverwood		5
*A.J. Hollioake	c Blakey b Silverwood	40	b Hamilton		40
A.W. Smith	c Byas b Robinson	0	lbw b Silverwood		3
#G.J. Kersey	c Byas b Silverwood	83	st Blakey b Stemp		20
R.W. Nowell	c Blakey b Robinson	10	b Stemp		6
C.G. Rackemann	c Bevan b Silverwood	0	b Silverwood		5
S.G. Kenlock	c Moxon b Robinson	7	c Byas b Silverwood		8
J.M. de la Pena	not out	0	not out		2
Extras	lb 10, w 3, nb 12	25	lb 4, nb 2		6
Total	**(all out)**	**409**	**(all out)**		**175**

YORKSHIRE

*M.D. Moxon	b Hollioake	63	c Nadeem Shahid		90
M.P. Vaughan	c Kersey b de la Pena	19	c & b Smith		38
D. Byas	c Butcher b Rackemann	30	[4] c Brown b Hollioake		15
M.G. Bevan	not out	153	[5] c Nadeem Shahid b Nowell		29
S.A. Kellett	c Kersey b Kenlock	28	[6] lbw b Rackemann		4
#R.J. Blakey	b Rackemann	9	[8] not out		12
G.M. Hamilton	b Rackemann	9	[8] not out		12
S.M. Milburn	c Kersey b Rackemann	2	[3] c Nadeem Shahid b Smith		0
C.E.W. Silverwood	b de la Pena	10	c Brown b Hollioake		9
R.D. Stemp	b de la Pena	0	c Nadeem Shahid b Hollioake		0
M.A. Robinson	b Rackemann	0	c Butcher b Hollioake		0
Extras	b 3, lb 6, w 1, nb 16	26	b 4, lb 2, w 2, nb 12		20
Total	**(all out)**	**366**	**(all out)**		**217**

Bowling

YORKSHIRE	O	M	R	W	O	M	R	W
Silverwood	22	3	94	3	16.1	2	62	5
Hamilton	14	2	72	1	8	1	29	1
Milburn	10	2	39	1	6	0	21	1
Robinson	24.4	8	64	4	12	4	22	0
Stemp	41	12	103	1	18	6	37	3
Vaughan	11	3	27	0				

SURREY	O	M	R	W	O	M	R	W
Rackemann	26.3	9	64	4	26	8	63	2
Kenlock	20	7	50	1	2	0	14	0
de la Pena	19	5	53	3	2	0	23	0
Smith	7	0	43	0	19	6	47	2
Nowell	23	6	66	0	17	7	41	2
Hollioake	12	1	49	1	10	2	22	4
Butcher	9	4	32	1				
Nadeem Shahid					2	1	1	0

FALL OF WICKETS

	S	Y	S	Y
1st	1	39	36	73
2nd	137	105	72	77
3rd	224	129	92	126
4th	279	187	96	185
5th	283	299	117	194
6th	328	312	138	194
7th	390	324	160	197
8th	400	355	165	215
9th	401	355	169	215
10th	409	366	175	217

Umpires: P.B. Wight and P. Willey

SURREY v. HAMPSHIRE

Date: 14-17 July 1999   **County Championship**
Location: Guildford

The return of their four Test match players, Mark Butcher, Alec Stewart, Graham Thorpe and Alex Tudor, enabled Surrey to field their full-strength side for the first time in the season. Jon Batty, Darren Bicknell, Jason Ratcliffe and Gary Butcher were the unlucky men to make way.

Surrey won the toss in their annual visit to Guildford, decided to bat, and were away to a dreadful start, Ian Ward being out bowled by Nixon McLean to the first ball he faced and Mark Butcher being caught and bowled by Peter Hartley in the next over to leave Surrey 7 for 2. Ben Hollioake looked to be justifying his promotion in the order, hitting Hartley for three boundaries through midwicket in 2 overs. Hopes of a recovery were dashed when Graham Thorpe top-edged an ambitious pull shot at Mclean and skied the ball to Derek Kenway at midwicket.

Alistair Brown, like Hollioake, was quickly into his stride with three well-struck boundaries but, with the score at 45, the Hampshire openers struck two further blows to leave the home side in a crisis situation. The younger Hollioake was caught at the wicket and Brown fell leg-before to McLean, so half the Surrey side were back in the pavilion inside 9 overs.

Alec Stewart and Adam Hollioake set out to retrieve the situation, although Stewart appeared determined to play his natural game, scoring two fours straight away. A tranquil phase followed and then Hartley switched ends to win a lbw verdict against Stewart with a ball that seemed to jag back and lift. Next ball Ian Salisbury was caught by the wicketkeeper Aymes. With Adam Hollioake constructing a sizeable innings Alex Tudor adopted the aggressive approach of his colleagues with three fours off the bowling of Hartley. Just before lunch Tudor's innings ended when he played on to Nixon McLean. After lunch the pace did

Graham Thorpe hits out against Gloucestershire in 2005. *(Empics)*

not slacken as Adam Hollioake progressed to a priceless half-century. Then Martin Bicknell was dismissed lbw and Hollioake tried to take command but Saqlain only lasted 2 balls for the innings to close on 171. In Hampshire's first innings Surrey needed a good start, which they achieved as Jason Laney was trapped in front by Martin Bicknell, with umpire Peter Willey completing an amazing personal sequence of three affirmative leg-before decisions in the space of five deliveries. Kendall and Kenway both gave unaccepted chances. Bicknell then won another lbw decision to remove Kendall but Kenway and Smith saw Hampshire out to tea at 88 for 2. In the evening session a few good balls went unrewarded but a wide short delivery brought Bicknell the wicket of Robin Smith as he carved the ball straight to Alistair Brown at third man. Kenway and Keech started to accumulate useful runs but 3 wickets fell in the closing overs to leave Hampshire at 166 for 6.

In the second over on day two, Kenway was caught at first slip but the lower Hampshire order then added 147 runs. Nixon McLean scored freely but his partnership with

Mark Butcher batting against Hampshire in 2005. *(Empics)*

Shaun Udal ended in unfortunate circumstances. Fending off a shortish delivery from Alex Tudor Udal took a nasty blow on the elbow, left the field in obvious distress and was taken to hospital. After lunch the Hampshire fast bowlers continued to hit boundaries but Hartley tried once too often and was caught off a skier by Alex Tudor. Udal then emerged from the pavilion with his arm in a sling under his sweater, but did not have to face a ball as McLean was out in the same Ben Hollioake over having scored a career-best 70 in 52 balls to help Hampshire complete a first-innings lead of 151.

Despite early alarms, Mark Butcher and Ian Ward got Surrey away to a good start in the second innings with an opening partnership of 107. A maiden first-class century for Ward eluded him as he clipped a full toss to midwicket, where Matthew Keech pulled off a fine catch leaping high to his right. Mark Butcher and Graham Thorpe then proceeded to compile another century partnership to bring Surrey back into the match. Butcher missed out on a century, being dismissed for 94 in an innings that lasted nearly four hours and contained fourteen fours.

Surrey made a poor start to the third day, losing 2 wickets in the first over bowled by Peter Hartley, night watchman Salisbury caught at square leg and Ben Hollioake caught at the wicket. Alistair Brown edged the last ball of the second over but the ball fell just short of the wicketkeeper. Thorpe and Brown took the score past 300 but then Brown fell to a slip catch bringing Alec Stewart to the wicket. He immediately looked in good touch and just before lunch Graham Thorpe reached his century. Alec Stewart is out to the

Surrey v. Hampshire

Martin Bicknell.

third ball of the afternoon session, gloving a low leg-side catch to Adrian Aymes. Adam Hollioake started where he left off on day one and with Thorpe rapidly increasing his boundary count the score began to climb at a healthy rate. Hollioake departed to a diving catch at cover after a 53-run stand and then Tudor was trapped lbw. Going for a second run to third man Thorpe was run out in a desperate sprint for the crease. Graham Thorpe received a huge ovation from the crowd for a match-turning innings of 164, which lasted for 277 balls spread over six-and-a-quarter hours. Martin Bicknell and Saqlain then added some 31 runs for the last wicket to set Hampshire the target of scoring 332 runs in four sessions.

Surrey presented their opponents with 15 extras before a run was scored from the bat. Bicknell then trapped Laney lbw for the second time in the match and a few runs later Kendall was dismissed in the same manner, again the same as the first innings. Hampshire hopes rise a little, but as Saqlain enters sthe attack the moment of truth arrived. With only his second ball Kenway fell to a bat-pad catch at short leg. With the score at 98 Keech was beaten by a quicker delivery and departed lbw to a ball that appeared to keep low. In the next over Ian Salisbury appeared to pin Robin Smith plumb lbw with a googly but the appeal was turned down.

Into the last morning and Saqlain was soon causing problems and in his second over he saw Thorpe miss a fairly straightforward catch at slip offered by night watchman Peter Hartley. In the next few overs Hartley was dropped again on two occasions, by Mark Butcher and Alex Tudor. Finally, a Bicknell delivery shot through very low to win a straightforward lbw verdict. Aymes then fell to a catch off Saqlain and, despite an attack by Stephenson, wickets fell quickly to give Surrey victory before lunch with Saqlain taking 6.

This was Surrey's seventh victory of the season, leaving them comfortably at the top of the championship table. They went on to become champions in style, winning 12 and drawing 4 of their 16 matches and having a margin of 57 points over Lancashire in second place.

SURREY *v.* HAMPSHIRE

Played at Guildford 14th, 15th, 16th and 17th July 1999 [4-day Match]   Toss: Surrey
Surrey won by 156 runs

SURREY

M.A. Butcher	c & b Hartley	1	c Stephenson b Hartley		94
I.J. Ward	b McLean	0	c Keech b Laney		55
G.P. Thorpe	c Kenway b McLean	4	run out		164
B.C. Hollioake	c Aymes b Hartley	15	(5) c Aymes b Hartley		0
A.D. Brown	lbw b McLean	17	(6) c Stephenson b Udal		40
#A.J. Stewart	lbw b Hartley	23	(7) c Aymes b McLean		19
*A.J. Hollioake	not out	63	(8) c Keech b Stephenson		23
I.D.K. Salisbury	c Aymes b Hartley	0	(4) c Keech b Hartley		12
A.J. Tudor	b McLean	17	lbw b Stephenson		0
M.P. Bicknell	lbw b Udal	15	c & b McLean		35
Saqlain Mushtaq	lbw b Udal	0	not out		10
Extras	lb 6, w 6, nb 4	16	b 5, lb 11, w 2, nb 12		30
Total	**(all out)**	**171**	**(all out)**		**482**

HAMPSHIRE

J.S. Laney	lbw b Bicknell	0	lbw b Bicknell		7
D.A. Kenway	c Thorpe b Bicknell	63	c Ward b Saqlain		20
W.S. Kendall	lbw b Bicknell	17	lbw b Bicknell		9
*R.A. Smith	c Brown b Bicknell	40	b Saqlain		46
M. Keech	lbw b Salisbury	11	lbw b Saqlain		8
#A.N. Aymes	lbw b Saqlain	1	(7) c Bicknell b Saqlain		5
J.P. Stephenson	c A.J. Hollioake b Salisbury	4	(8) lbw b Saqlain		26
A.D. Mascarenhas	b Tudor	26	(9) c Stewart b Salisbury		5
S.D. Udal	not out	30	(11) not out		0
N.A.M. McLean	c Butcher b B.C. Hollioake	70	lbw b Saqlain		4
P.J. Hartley	c Tudor b B.C. Hollioake	15	(6) lbw b Bicknell		17
Extras	b4, lb 17, w 8, nb 16	45	b9, lb 13, w 6		28
Total	**(all out)**	**322**	**(all out)**		**175**

Bowling

HAMPSHIRE	O	M	R	W	O	M	R	W
McLean	12	1	63	4	30.4	0	118	2
Hartley	17	6	66	4	31	8	88	3
Mascarenhas	9	2	26	0	19	7	50	0
Stephenson	2	0	8	0	27	0	132	2
Udal	1.3	0	2	2	16	2	46	1
Laney					12	2	32	1

SURREY	O	M	R	W	O	M	R	W
Bicknell	24	5	75	4	17	3	50	3
Tudor	17	2	69	1	6	1	16	0
Saqlain Mushtaq	28	10	77	1	17	3	44	6
B.C. Hollioake	5.5	0	31	2	4	0	17	0
Salisbury	15	3	45	2	7.1	2	19	1
Butcher	2	0	4	0	5	3	7	0

FALL OF WICKETS

	S	H	S	H
1st	1	0	107	26
2nd	7	38	225	44
3rd	27	116	239	74
4th	45	160	239	98
5th	45	161	304	129
6th	74	166	343	134
7th	74	175	396	162
8th	117	223	402	171
9th	157	318	451	175
10th	171	322	482	175

Umpires: B. Leadbeater and P. Willey

SURREY v. HAMPSHIRE

Date: 1-4 June 2000   County Championship
Location: The Fosters Oval

This match started with the situation that the losing side would drop to the bottom of Division One and the winners would move up to fourth place. It proved to be a most dramatic match that went to an almost unbearable tense finish rarely seen at The Oval.

The number of spectators witnessing the match was so small that one wondered about the future of county cricket when a match was featuring the County Champions and the only one of *Wisden's* Five Cricketers of the Century still playing the game, Shane Warne, and it still only managed to attract a first-morning attendance that barely ran into double figures.

Not for the first time Surrey batted right down the order, having won the toss and elected to bat. Wickets fell regularly but Graham Thorpe fashioned a typical half-century. Just after tea on the first day they lost their sixth wicket at 166 but Bicknell joined Batty to start a recovery. Martin Bicknell scored an impressive fifty and then Alex Tudor came to the wicket to complete a blistering innings of 64 not out. In the Hampshire first innings, Bicknell took 3 quick wickets but Giles White, aided by Adrian Aymes, steadied the ship, taking the score from 33 for 3 to 143 for 4. Alex Tudor and Saqlain Mushtaq then combined to bring Surrey back into the match, with White falling just 4 runs short of a century. Hampshire were left 123 runs behind Surrey on the first innings, but struck back initially with Alan Mullally taking early wickets and then Shane Warne showing his craft by taking 5 wickets in 21.1 overs with 7 maidens. Only Adam Hollioake could offer any substantial resistance as Surrey were dismissed for 142.

Hampshire needed 266 runs to win in four sessions with a minimum of 130 overs left for play. All results were possible. Laney fell to Tudor for his second duck of the match and White was stumped off Ian Salisbury, leaving Hampshire on 58 for 2 from 34 tense and tight overs at the close of play.

As the final day got under way, Surrey's bowlers rose to the challenge and wickets fell quickly to leave Hampshire on 87 for 6. From this seemingly hopeless position, Warne launched a counterattack that briefly unsettled Surrey until Tudor struck again by having Kendall taken at slip shortly before lunch with the score on

Alex Tudor bowling against Nottinghamshire in 2003.
(Empics)

125. After the break Warne was caught and bowled by Saqlain with the visitors still 105 runs short of victory. When Mullally followed him back to the pavilion 12 runs later a win for Surrey seemed assured as Dimitri Mascarenhas was carrying an injury and last man Simon Francis had a career-best score of 11.

Francis immediately looked a more capable batsman than Mullally and settled in to play a sensible second fiddle to Mascarenhas. Various milestones were passed, Francis' career-best, the fifty partnership, Mascarenhas's half-century and a new record partnership for Hampshire's last wicket against Surrey, as the batsmen edged their team closer to a highly unlikely victory. At tea only 5 runs were required for an amazing win. When play resumed, 2 tense overs and two singles to Mascarenhas followed before the decisive over from Tudor arrived. Having missed out on a short, wide delivery first ball and then mistimed a drive to mid-on from the second ball, Mascarenhas then attempted to pull the next delivery, only to mistime the stroke horribly and dolly a simple catch back to the bowler. This left Surrey the winners by the small margin of 2 runs.

SURREY v. HAMPSHIRE

Played at The Foster's Oval on 1st, 2nd, 3rd and 4th June 2000 [4-day Match]　　　Toss: Surrey
Surrey won by 2 runs

SURREY

M.A. Butcher	run out	32	c Warne b Mullally	2
I.J. Ward	c Warne b Francis	5	c Aymes b Francis	0
G.P. Thorpe	lbw b Stephenson	58	lbw b Mullally	13
*A.J. Hollioake	lbw b Stephenson	37	b Warne	41
A.D. Brown	c sub b Mullally	24	b Mullally	7
J.D. Ratcliffe	b Warne	0	b Warne	26
#J.N. Batty	c Kendall b Francis	16	c Stephenson b Warne	9
M.P. Bicknell	b Francis	59	lbw b Mullally	14
I.D.K. Salisbury	c Kenway b Francis	1	(10) not out	8
A.J. Tudor	not out	64	(9) c Laney b Warne	0
Saqlain Mushtaq	lbw b Warne	21	c Aymes b Warne	10
Extras	b 1, lb 9, w 4, nb 2	16	b 2, lb 4, w 4, nb 2	12
Total	**(all out)**	**333**	**(all out)**	**142**

HAMPSHIRE

G.W.White	c Ward b Saqlain	96	st Batty b Salisbury	23
J.S. Laney	c Brown b Bicknell	0	c Hollioake b Tudor	0
W.S. Kendall	c Thorpe b Bicknell	7	c Thorpe b Tudor	41
*R.A. Smith	c Batty b Bicknell	0	c Butcher b Bicknell	12
D.A. Kenway	c Brown b Tudor	12	c Hollioake b Tudor	1
#A.N. Aymes	c Hollioake b Tudor	44	c Batty b Tudor	2
J.P. Stephenson	c Thorpe b Saqlain	6	c Hollioake b Saqlain	1
S.K. Warne	b Tudor	19	c & b Saqlain	50
A.D. Mascarenhas	c Brown b Bicknell	2	c & b Tudor	59
A.D. Mullally	not out	8	c Ratcliffe b Saqlain	4
S.R.G. Francis	c Hollioake b Saqlain	2	not out	30
Extras	b 6, lb 2, w 2, nb 4	14	b 7, lb 19, nb 14	40
Total	**(all out)**	**210**	**(all out)**	**263**

Bowling

HAMPSHIRE	O	M	R	W	O	M	R	W
Mullally	23	8	43	1	17	5	31	4
Francis	23	5	95	4	10	0	58	1
Mascarenhas	14	6	30	0				
Stephenson	20	4	74	2	9	4	16	0
Warne	30.1	9	81	2	21.1	7	31	5

SURREY	O	M	R	W	O	M	R	W
Bicknell	29	12	52	4	26	8	60	1
Tudor	16	5	52	3	19.3	8	57	5
Saqlain Mushtaq	34	10	65	3	44	15	89	3
Salisbury	13	4	33	0	16	7	31	1

FALL OF WICKETS

	S	H	S	H
1st	6	9	4	4
2nd	79	33	4	40
3rd	124	33	24	74
4th	153	73	44	84
5th	156	151	90	86
6th	166	161	106	87
7th	207	193	109	125
8th	215	198	121	161
9th	278	207	131	173
10th	333	210	142	263

Umpires: J.W. Holder and K.E. Palmer

SURREY v. LEICESTERSHIRE

Date: 7-9 July 2000   **County Championship**

Location: Oakham School

First-class cricket made a triumphant return to Oakham School after sixty-two years in July 2000. Attendances were excellent, the pitch played fast and true, and much of the cricket – at least from Surrey – matched the delightful setting.

But for Leicestershire there was an unwelcome symmetry with their last Championship game here, in 1938. They followed on and crashed to a heavy defeat. Then, Bryan Valentine made 242 for Kent; now, Brown scored a career-best 295 not out for Surrey. Though he gave four chances it was a splendid innings. He batted eight hours and thirty-seven minutes, faced 392 balls and hit thirty-two fours and a six. This innings of Alistair Brown was the sixth-highest ever scored for Surrey.

Surrey had not started well, losing the wicket of Mark Butcher without a run on the board. Ian Ward and Adam Hollioake did not last long but Nadeem Shahid and Brown saw Surrey through to lunch on 112 for 3. Wickets fell regularly during the afternoon to leave Surrey on 190 for 7 shortly after Brown reached his century from 139 balls. But Brown found stauncher allies in the tail and shared two partnerships of 141, first with Tudor and then, for the tenth wicket, with Saqlain Mushtaq, who hit his maiden Championship fifty. At the end of the first day Surrey were 334 for 8 and, on the second morning, despite the new ball having been taken, runs came easily and Saqlain was outscoring Brown. After completing his fifty, Saqlain was mortified to be bowled by Wells, thereby denying Brown the chance of scoring his maiden triple-century. Nevertheless the last 3 Surrey wickets had added 315 runs.

The crowd's generous applause for Brown's superb innings was still fresh in the memory when the home side's openers emerged from the pavilion to start a reply that was, incredibly, almost over by tea. With Bicknell and Tudor picking up 3 wickets apiece and Ben Smith running himself out in attempting a sharp single, Leicestershire flopped to 51 for 7, still 305 runs short of avoiding the follow-on and suddenly on course for a crushing defeat. Neil Burns and Philip DeFreitas rallied their team briefly but Leicestershire finished the day at 134 for 9.

Alistair Brown – compiler of Surrey's highest individual scores in recent years. *(Empics)*

The next morning Leicestershire were immediately in trouble as they followed on 362 runs behind and lost Darren Maddy first ball, caught by Batty off Bicknell. By lunch they were 42 for 4, looking set for a three-day defeat, but rain kept the players off the field for two hours. Since the skies were grey and the weather forecast for the final day was poor, there was suddenly a degree of concern in the Surrey ranks.

When play resumed at 4 p.m., Ben Smith's early departure was followed by the hosts' most protracted resistance of the match, as Darren Stevens, scoring 68 from 80 balls, was supported by Chris Lewis and DeFreitas. Saqlain then took vital wickets as drizzle began to turn to rain. Surrey had won, just in the nick of time, by an innings and 178 runs. This third successive victory lifted them to the top of the table – where they would stay for the rest of the season to be crowned County Champions.

SURREY v. LEICESTERSHIRE

Played at Oakham School on 7th, 8th and 9th July 2000 [4-day Match]　　　Toss: Surrey
Surrey won by an innings and 178 runs

SURREY

M.A. Butcher	c Wells b Ormond	0
I.J. Ward	lbw b Ormond	6
N. Shahid	c Burns b DeFreitas	37
*A.J. Hollioake	c Lewis b Ormond	4
A.D. Brown	not out	295
B.C. Hollioake	c Habib b DeFreitas	2
#J.N. Batty	c Lewis b Maddy	19
M.P. Bicknell	c Burns b Lewis	5
A.J. Tudor	c Maddy b Wells	22
I.D.K. Salisbury	c Maddy b DeFreitas	12
Saqlain Mushtaq	b Wells	66
Extras	b 3, lb 10, w 2, nb 22	37
Total	**(all out)**	**505**

LEICESTERSHIRE

D.L. Maddy	c A.J. Hollioake b Bicknell	10	c Batty b Bicknell		0
I.J. Sutcliffe	c Brown b Tudor	1	c Batty b B.C. Hollioake		14
*V.J. Wells	c Saqlain b Tudor	13	b Bicknell		9
B.F. Smith	run out	3	c Brown b Bicknell		20
A. Habib	c Brown b Bicknell	0	st Batty b Saqlain		4
D.I. Stevens	lbw b Tudor	6	b Saqlain		68
C.C. Lewis	lbw b Bicknell	3	c Batty b B.C. Hollioake		24
P.A.J. DeFreitas	c A.J. Hollioake b Saqlain	38	not out		25
#N.D. Burns	c A.J. Hollioake b Saqlain	30	c Batty b Saqlain		8
A. Kumble	b Salisbury	10	c A.J. Hollioake b Saqlain		0
J. Ormond	not out	5	lbw b Saqlain		0
Extras	b2, lb 12, nb 10	24	b5, lb 3, nb 4		12
Total	**(all out)**	**143**	**(all out)**		**184**

Bowling

LEICESTERSHIRE	O	M	R	W
Ormond	34	4	92	3
DeFreitas	29	6	115	3
Kumble	35	5	101	0
Lewis	18	2	60	1
Wells	17.5	1	65	2
Maddy	15	2	59	1

SURREY	O	M	R	W	O	M	R	W
Bicknell	11	3	41	3	15	4	44	3
Tudor	11	6	34	3				
Salisbury	18	8	29	1	14	4	41	0
Saqlain	17.2	8	25	2	15	4	35	5
B.C. Hollioake					15	4	48	2
Brown					1	0	8	0

FALL OF WICKETS

	S	L	L
1st	0	12	0
2nd	11	12	22
3rd	25	27	26
4th	113	27	40
5th	125	44	56
6th	181	49	118
7th	190	51	149
8th	331	106	182
9th	364	131	184
10th	505	143	184

Umpires: A. Clarkson and J.W. Holder

SURREY v. LEICESTERSHIRE

Date: 19-21 July 2000   County Championship
Location: Guildford

Two weeks after their defeat at Oakham School, Leicestershire came to Guildford. Martin Bicknell, on his home ground, turned the game on its head with the best match return in England since 1956 and the best by a fast bowler since 1952. But the bare figures, 16 for 119, scarcely capture the drama of his superb seam and swing bowling on a near-perfect pitch.

Winning the toss Leicestershire decided to bat. Bicknell managed two strikes with the new ball but with Carl Greenidge, deputising for the injured Alex Tudor, unable to break through at the other end, Iain Sutcliffe and Ben Smith stabilised the innings until lunch. Bicknell picked up another wicket after the break, Sutcliffe, but Smith shared two further fifty-plus stands before completing a fine century from 182 balls shortly before tea. He was then caught at slip from the fourth delivery of the final session but Phillip DeFreitas and Dominic Williamson added 86 for the eighth wicket. The next morning the Leicestershire innings closed on 318 as Bicknell had Kumble caught at the wicket and returned innings figures of 7 for 72.

Mark Butcher was given out caught down the legside from the third ball of the Surrey reply. Nadeem Shahid then played very attractively in partnership with Ian Ward before falling to Kumble on the stroke of lunch. The middle-order batting was unable to produce many runs and for a time Alistair Brown was forced to retire temporarily after taking a nasty blow on the wrist from Ormond. Meanwhile, Ian Ward went on to reach his century from 206 balls after almost five hours of impressive concentration. After his dismissal, 4 wickets fell in 5 overs and Leicestershire finished with a first-innings lead of 30. Jimmy Ormond finished with 6 wickets and in 2002 joined the Surrey staff.

Any sense of contentment that the visitors felt after regaining the initiative was to be wiped away before stumps were drawn. Maddy was bowled by Bicknell with an absolute peach of a delivery with the innings just 6 balls old. Sutcliffe lost his middle stump from the fourth ball of Bicknell's next over. Three wickets fell as the score slipped from 31 for 2 to 33 for 5. Bicknell took all 3, Stevens and Habib both being caught

Martin Bicknell bowling against Warwickshire at Whitgift School in 2005. *(Empics)*

at second slip and Burns trapped lbw. Greenidge dismissed Smith just before the close, which left Leicestershire on 33 for 6.

Forty-seven runs were added the next morning by Vince Wells and DeFreitas before Bicknell began a spell of bowling to pick up the last 4 wickets and give him figures of 9 for 47 for the innings, leaving Surrey the task of scoring 118 for victory. Butcher knocked 53 off the target in 19 overs before lunch and then completed the win in a further 20 overs after the break.

Leicestershire's first-innings 318 was the highest total Surrey had conceded to date in the season and the second innings of 87 was the lowest.

Martin Bicknell has been a great servant for Surrey and during 2005 achieved a great landmark by taking his 1,000th wicket for the county to join a very select band of fine bowlers. With the change in the number of first-class matches now played his achievement is unlikely to be matched or repeated in the future.

The season of 2000 saw the introduction of two divisions in the County Championship. Having to play the other eight teams twice, Surrey became champions, winning 9 matches under the captaincy of Adam Hollioake.

SURREY *v.* LEICESTERSHIRE

SURREY *v.* LEICESTERSHIRE

Played at Guildford on 19th, 20th and 21st July 2000 [4-day Match]   Toss: Leicestershire
Surrey won by 10 wickets

LEICESTERSHIRE

D.L. Maddy	c Batty b Bicknell	3	b Bicknell		0
I.J. Sutcliffe	c Brown b Bicknell	37	b Bicknell		7
D.I. Stevens	c & b Bicknell	6	[4] c Butcher b Bicknell		14
B.F. Smith	c Butcher b Bicknell	102	[3] lbw b Greenidge		8
A. Habib	c Shahid b Saqlain	20	[6] c Butcher b Bicknell		2
*V.J. Wells	lbw b Bicknell	15	[7] c Brown b Bicknell		17
P.A.J. DeFreitas	c A.J. Hollioake b Saqlain	27	[8] c Butcher b Bicknell		24
#N.D. Burns	c Batty b Bicknell	4	[5] lbw b Bicknell		0
D. Williamson	c Batty b A.J. Hollioake	47	not out		1
A. Kumble	c Batty b Bicknell	2	c B.C. Hollioake b Bicknell		5
J. Ormond	not out	2	b Bicknell		0
Extras	b4, lb 23, nb 26	53	lb 3, nb 4, w 2		9
Total	**(all out)**	**318**	**(all out)**		**87**

SURREY

M.A. Butcher	c Burns b Ormond	0	not out	47
I.J. Ward	c Habib b DeFreitas	107	not out	61
N. Shahid	c Smith b Kumble	47		
*A.J. Hollioake	c DeFreitas b Ormond	18		
A.D. Brown	c Burns b Ormond	34		
B.C. Hollioake	c Sutcliffe b Ormond	21		
#J.N. Batty	c Habib b Kumble	3		
M.P. Bicknell	lbw b Ormond	0		
I.D.K. Salisbury	not out	10		
Saqlain Mushtaq	c Habib b Ormond	1		
C.G. Greenidge	lbw b Kumble	6		
Extras	b 12, lb 3, w 4, nb 22	41	b 3, lb 6, nb 2	11
Total	**(all out)**	**288**	**(for no wicket)**	**119**

Bowling

SURREY	O	M	R	W	O	M	R	W
Bicknell	28.1	5	72	7	12.5	3	47	9
Greenidge	12	2	35	0	11	6	35	1
B.C. Hollioake	19	5	74	0				
Saqlain Mushtaq	39	9	93	2	1	0	2	0
A.J. Hollioake	4	2	8	1				
Salisbury	6	1	9	0				

LEICESTERSHIRE	O	M	R	W	O	M	R	W
Ormond	29	6	87	6	3	1	14	0
DeFreitas	25	7	76	1	15	2	30	0
Wells	4	0	25	0	4	1	13	0
Williamson	6	0	17	0	7	2	17	0
Kumble	17	1	68	3	3	1	5	0
Maddy					3	0	11	0
Stevens					3	0	8	0
Sutcliffe					1.3	0	12	0

FALL OF WICKETS

	L	S	L
1st	16	2	0
2nd	26	93	7
3rd	95	123	31
4th	146	198	31
5th	199	209	33
6th	214	266	33
7th	226	270	80
8th	312	272	81
9th	312	273	87
10th	318	288	87

Umpires: V.A. Holder and N.A. Mallender

SURREY v. LEICESTERSHIRE

Date: 4-7 July 2001   County Championship
Location: Leicester

For this match Surrey were short of five regular players, Alec Stewart, Ian Ward and Mark Butcher being on Test match duty and Graham Thorpe and Mark Ramprakash being injured. Nadeem Shahid and Gary Butcher came into the side with Michael Carberry making his first-class debut.

By the end of the first day, this game had ostensibly run more than half its course despite a blameless pitch. Twenty wickets had fallen and Leicestershire, 79 for 0 in their second innings enjoyed a lead of 142. Surrey had dismissed their hosts for 165 in 43 overs, with Trevor Ward providing the only top-order resistance as his side slipped to 88 for 7. By the end of the afternoon Surrey had been dismissed for 102 in 38 overs with Devon Malcolm claiming his best County Championship figures of 8 wickets for 63 by using a combination of pace and swing to take advantage of some inept batting.

Leicestershire then batted for most of the second day under a scorching sun, completing 472 for 8 before declaring and setting Surrey the small matter of 536 to win with a little more than two days of the match to win. Ben Smith then compiled a solidly impressive 179 and was supported by Daniel Marsh and Neil Burns. Surrey were hampered by the absence of Ian Salisbury, who had broken his toe and owed a debt of gratitude to Saqlain Mushtaq, who bowled 47 overs unchanged.

Having ended the second day on 28 for 1 Surrey batted gamely through a grim and grey third day that was shorn of 27 overs by rain and bad light, though defeat still looked on the cards at 281 for 6. This was in spite of battling efforts from first Adam and Ben Hollioake who added 103 for the fourth wicket, and then Gary Butcher and Alex Tudor, who were unbeaten at the end of the day having batted through the last 25 overs.

The last day turned out to be every bit as cloudy and unsettled as the previous day, though the first rainfall came just a couple of minutes too late to save Gary Butcher with the score on 318 for 7. After 11 overs had been lost to rain Surrey looked likely to get through to lunch without losing another wicket until Alex

Saqlain Mushtaq bowling against Derbyshire in 2003. *(Empics)*

Tudor's marvellously determined innings of 86 from 148 balls came to an end when he was bowled by DeFreitas armed with the new ball. Another shower delayed the restart and with nobody sure whether Salisbury would bat the chances of Surrey surviving looked very slim. Jonathan Batty and Martin Bicknell were facing a seemingly lost cause, and the end appeared nigh when Batty was unluckily bowled off his thigh pad with 39 overs still to be bowled. The prospect of further rain was the only thing that kept hopes alive as Salisbury hobbled out to the crease with a runner, though the last-wicket pair were still together at 3.30 p.m., with the score on 424 for 9 when another heavy downpour sent the players scurrying off for an early tea.

When play resumed at 4.20 p.m. some 25 overs and 3 balls remained to be bowled. Devon Malcolm switched to round the wicket in an attempt to soften up the batsmen, though Bicknell and Salisbury were sufficiently well set to deal with this as they took the score past 450 and then completed a hundred partnership. Despite one or two scares they saw out the game to ensure Surrey earned a draw to extend an unbeaten run to 18 games. The fourth-innings total was the third highest ever in the history of the County Championship.

SURREY *v.* LEICESTERSHIRE

Played at Leicester on 4th, 5th, 6th and 7th July 2001 [4-day Match]   Toss: Leicestershire
Match drawn

LEICESTERSHIRE

Batsman	Dismissal	R		Dismissal	R
T.R.Ward	c Shahid b Saqlain	46		c A.J. Hollioake b Saqlain	42
I.J.Sutcliffe	c Shahid b Bicknell	0		b Bicknell	25
B.F.Smith	c & b Bicknell	6		c Brown b Butcher	179
D.J.Marsh	c B.C. Hollioake b Bicknell	1		st Batty b Saqlain	82
A.Habib	c A.J. Hollioake b Saqlain	3		c B.C. Hollioake b Saqlain	5
D.L.Maddy	c B.C. Hollioake b Tudor	1		c Shahid b Saqlain	0
*V.J.Wells	lbw b Tudor	14		c B.C. Hollioake b A.J. Hollioake	32
#N.D.Burns	lbw b Saqlain	14		not out	66
P.A.J.DeFreitas	lbw b Saqlain	22		c Batty b Saqlain	3
J.Ormond	not out	14			
D.E.Malcolm	c A.J. Hollioake b Bicknell	3			
Extras	lb 6, nb 4	10		b8, lb 3, nb 22, p 5	38
Total	**(all out)**	**165**		**(for 8 wickets declared)**	**472**

SURREY

Batsman	Dismissal	R		Dismissal	R
N. Shahid	c Smith b Malcolm	7		c Ward b Malcolm	14
M.A. Carberry	lbw b DeFreitas	23		c Burns b DeFreitas	13
B.C. Hollioake	b Malcolm	0		(4) b Ormond	59
*A.J. Hollioake	lbw b Malcolm	0		(5) b Wells	64
A.D. Brown	c Habib b Malcolm	15		(6) c Burns b Ormond	5
G.P. Butcher	lbw b DeFreitas	9		(7) b Marsh	38
A.J. Tudor	c Burns b Malcolm	13		(8) b DeFreitas	86
#J.N. Batty	c Habib b Malcolm	0		(9) b Malcolm	12
M.P. Bicknell	b Malcolm	12		(10) not out	85
I.D.K. Salisbury	c Marsh b Malcolm	15		(11) not out	30
Saqlain Mushtaq	not out	5		(3) lbw b Marsh	4
Extras	lb 1, nb 2	3		b 23, lb 31, w 10, nb 4	68
Total	**(all out)**	**102**		**(for 9 wickets)**	**478**

Bowling

SURREY	O	M	R	W	O	M	R	W
Bicknell	15	4	54	4	23	6	69	1
Tudor	11	4	45	2	8	1	52	0
Saqlain Mushtaq	17	4	60	4	52.2	9	172	5
B.C. Hollioake					6	0	41	0
Butcher					13	3	53	1
A.J. Hollioake					8	0	51	0
Brown					3	0	18	0

LEICESTERSHIRE	O	M	R	W	O	M	R	W
Ormond	12	3	25	0	30	8	72	2
Malcolm	18	3	63	8	43	12	124	2
DeFreitas	7	4	13	2	23	6	71	2
Marsh	1	1	0	0	30	11	76	2
Maddy					7	2	21	0
Wells					16	2	56	1
Sutcliffe					3	1	4	0

FALL OF WICKETS

	L	S	L	S
1st	3	11	79	20
2nd	23	11	93	35
3rd	25	11	260	55
4th	60	31	268	158
5th	61	56	268	170
6th	63	61	347	190
7th	88	62	455	318
8th	135	78	472	343
9th	154	87	–	369
10th	165	102	–	–

Umpires: A. Clarkson and V.A. Holder

SURREY v. GLAMORGAN

Date: 19 June 2002   Cheltenham & Gloucester Trophy
Location: The AMP Oval

At the time this was probably the most incredible limited-overs match ever played at first-class level, with no fewer than seven world records being smashed and countless United Kingdom, competition, club and personal records also perishing in an incredible blaze of strokeplay on a magnificent Oval pitch. Alistair Brown was the catalyst with an awesome, record-shattering innings of 268, leading Surrey to a seemingly insurmountable score of 438 for 5 that plucky Glamorgan challenged with centuries from Robert Croft and David Hemp, falling only 10 runs short of what would have been a breathtaking victory at the end of an unbelievable day's entertainment.

After a relative sedate start, with his personal tally being 19 out of a total of 35 for 0 at the end of the seventh over, Brown's innings really took off with three fours in the following over, bowled by Andrew Davis. Thereafter, he was simply unstoppable, offering just one awkward chance to wicketkeeper Mark Wallace with his score on 47, as he marched into the history books, trampling all over a host of records along the way.

Brown's fellow opener Ian Ward also batted quite superbly, even though his innings was understandably overshadowed by his partner's phenomenal knock. A magnificent opening partnership, which grew to 286 in 35 overs before Robert Croft sneaked a ball through Ward's defences, broke a number of records all on its own. By this stage of the Surrey innings, Brown had already surpassed his previous best score in this competition (72 v. Holland at The Oval in 1996) by the small matter of 99 runs, and there was no time to pause for breath as he went on to convert an 80-ball century into a sensational 134-ball double-ton, thereby becoming the first man to record two first-class limited-overs scores in excess of 200. Although there was a short boundary down towards the gasholders, many of the fours by Brown came from booming extra-cover drives to the longer boundary, and any six that crossed the rope on the shorter side usually ended up disappearing out of the ground in any case.

Alistair Brown in front of the scoreboard displaying his world record of 268. *(Empics)*

Once he had sailed past Alvin Kallicharran's 206 against Oxfordshire at Edgbaston in 1984 to claim the record for the highest individual one-day score ever registered in the United Kingdom, Brown's next goal – though there were few people in the ground who knew it – was Graeme Pollock's twenty-seven-year-old world-record individual tally of 222 not out, scored for Eastern Province against Border at East London. This mark was duly achieved in the forty-sixth over, with the score at this stage already an incredible 381 for 3, and by the time Brown fell to the first ball of the final over, departing to a hero's reception from the fairly small crowd, he had stormed on to his new world-best score of 268 from 160 balls, with twelve sixes and thirty fours. This stunning innings pushed the Surrey total up to a world-breaking 438 for 5 and, though all the bowlers suffered grievously at Brown's hand, none was more harshly treated than Darren Thomas, who set an unwanted new world mark for the most expensive bowling figures in returning 9-1-108-3.

SURREY v. GLAMORGAN

Ian Ward batting against Leicestershire in 2003. *(Empics)*

Facing the 'mission impossible' task of scoring 439 to win, Glamorgan made a rapid start through Croft as he smashed Martin Bicknell's first five deliveries of the innings for four on his way to a 22-ball fifty that saw the visitors' score racing up to 76 for 0 after just 6 overs. With nothing to lose, Croft continued to take advantage of some indifferent Surrey seam bowling to convert his half-century into Glamorgan's fastest-ever limited-overs hundred, as he reached the landmark from just 56 deliveries.

It appeared that the home side might just have a game on their hands after all as the score rushed along to 145 for 1 by the time the fielding restrictions were lifted after 15 overs and, though the visitors' stand-in skipper departed shortly afterwards for a glorious 69-ball 119, the pace barely slackened at all.

A quick-fire innings of 49 by Adrian Dale kept Glamorgan very much in contention during a stand of 98 for the fourth wicket with David Hemp, but even when Adam Hollioake struck twice in 3 balls to remove Dale and the dangerous Mike Powell, the Welsh dragon kept on breathing fire. With Hemp picking up steam after a relatively slow start and even the normally reliable Saqlain appearing to be cannon fodder in the prevailing conditions, Surrey's concerns grew, and with 10 overs to go the gutsy visitors needed 103 with 5 wickets remaining, and another world record had fallen – the highest match aggregate for any first-class limited-overs encounter. Luckily for Surrey, Hemp fell to Bicknell almost immediately after completing his excellent 85-ball century, and when the home side's senior bowler then also disposed of Wallace in his next over it looked like the Glamorgan storm might just be blowing out at 352 for 7.

SURREY v. GLAMORGAN

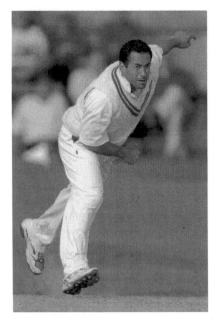

Adam Hollioake bowling against
Staffordshire in 2003. *(Empics)*

Not a bit of it. Desperate to atone for his nightmare with the ball, Darren Thomas blazed away, finding a reliable ally in Michael Kasprowicz and racing to a defiant half-century from just 30 balls to put the game back in the balance. With 44 needed from the last 4 overs, Ed Giddins then came up with a tight 7-run over, and when Kasprowicz was run out 2 overs later, leaving 22 to be scored from 9 balls, it finally looked like curtains for the Welshmen.

Since only five runs had accrued from the penultimate over of the match, bowled by Giddins, Glamorgan were therefore left needing 19 runs from the last over, which proved to be a bridge too far against the experienced Hollioake, who was playing his first game at The AMP Oval in the 2002 season. Cleaning up Andrew Davies, courtesy of a catch at wide mid-on, and Dean Cosker, with an off stump yorker, the Surrey captain ended with figures of 5 for 77 to see his side safely into the quarter-finals by the astonishingly slender margin of 9 runs.

The seven world records broken in this exceptional match were:

Highest team total in any limited-overs match
Highest team total by a side batting second in any limited-overs match
Highest individual score in any limited-overs match
Most boundaries in an innings by an individual in any limited-overs match
Most double-centuries scored by an individual in first-class limited-overs cricket
Highest run aggregate in any limited-overs match
Most expensive bowling analysis in any limited-overs match

The full details of this remarkable match have been recalled in great detail in a book entitled *268 – The Blow-by-Blow Account of Ali's Amazing Onslaught and the Day the Records Tumbled* by Trevor Jones, published by Sporting Declarations Books.

SURREY v. GLAMORGAN
[Cheltenham and Gloucester Trophy]

Played at The AMP Oval on 19th June 2002 [1-day Match]   Toss: Surrey
Surrey won by 9 runs

SURREY

I.J. Ward	b Croft	97
A.D. Brown	b Kasprowicz	268
M.R. Ramprakash	c & b S.D. Thomas	26
R. Clarke	c Wallace b S.D. Thomas	5
*A.J. Hollioake	c I.J. Thomas b S.D. Thomas	4
A.J. Stewart	not out	2
#J.N. Batty	not out	6
M.P. Bicknell		
Saqlain Mushtaq		
J. Ormond		
E.S.H. Giddins		
Extras	lb 8, w 20, nb 2	30
Total	**(for 5 wickets – 50 overs)**	**438**

GLAMORGAN

*R.D.B. Croft	c Ward b Hollioake	119
I.J. Thomas	run out (Hollioake)	23
D.L. Hemp	c Ormond b Bicknell	102
M.P. Maynard	c Ramprakash b Giddins	21
A. Dale	c Clarke b Hollioake	49
M.J. Powell	c Giddins b Hollioake	0
S.D. Thomas	not out	71
#M.A. Wallace	c Ramprakash b Bicknell	5
M.S. Kasprowicz	run out (Hollioake/Giddins)	25
A.P. Davies	c Ormond b Hollioake	1
D.A. Cosker	b Hollioake	0
Extras	lb 7, w 6	13
Total	**(all out, 49.5 overs)**	**429**

Bowling

GLAMORGAN	O	M	R	W
Kasprowicz	10	0	53	1
Davies	8	0	88	0
S.D. Thomas	9	0	108	3
Croft	8	0	62	1
Dale	8	0	68	0
Cosker	7	0	51	0

SURREY	O	M	R	W
Bicknell	10	0	84	2
Giddins	8	0	77	1
Ormond	9	0	72	0
Saqlain Mushtaq	10	0	82	0
Hollioake	8.5	0	77	5
Clarke	4	0	30	0

FALL OF WICKETS

	S	G
1st	286	113
2nd	354	162
3rd	376	197
4th	424	295
5th	431	295
6th	–	336
7th	–	352
8th	–	417
9th	–	421
10th	–	429

Umpires: I.J. Gould and P. Willey

SURREY v. KENT

Date: 19-22 July 2002   **County Championship**

Location: Canterbury

This was a fixture that began in controversy as Surrey disregarded England's request that Graham Thorpe be given match practice. Although Alec Stewart (rested) and Alex Tudor (shin splints) were to miss the match at England's behest, Mark Butcher had been promised a run-out ahead of the forthcoming First Test against India in order to assess the strength of his knee following recent surgery.

A good result at Canterbury against one of the other Championship hopefuls would go a long way towards getting Surrey back on track, though history was not in their favour – they hadn't won at the St Lawrence ground since 1989.

The match ended in triumph for Surrey as Ian Ward's eight-hour vigil, with solid support from Rikki Clarke, Saqlain Mushtaq and James Ormond, saw Surrey to an extraordinary victory after they had only narrowly, thanks to Hollioake's century, avoided the possibility of being asked to follow-on and then had to play the extra half-hour as Kent sought to wrap up the match on the third day. It was Surrey's highest fourth innings score to win a match, Ward's innings surpassed his ultimately less-meaningful career best, made on the same ground two years previously and the Ward-Ormond partnership replaced a ninety-six-year-old record against Kent, which left one wondering whether Surrey folk will talk with the same awe of Ward and Ormond as they do of Hayward and Strudwick. In all, 202 runs were scored after the seventh wicket fell, the most runs ever added for Surrey to win a match in these circumstances.

On a glorious sunny morning on the first day, with over 2,000 people in the ground, Kent won the toss. David Fulton and Robert Key gave Kent a good start with a century stand, although Surrey's early bowling and catching let them down, but just before lunch both opening batsmen fell to Saqlain in the space of 12 balls. Ed Smith and Andrew Symonds took the attack to Surrey immediately after lunch but, on 155, Smith was run out going for an unlikely run. James Hockley joined Symonds to pile on the pressure, adding over 100 until falling to Salisbury 4 short of his maiden half-century. The Australian Andrew Symonds, a great

Ian Ward hits a four as Michael Yardy takes evasive action in the match against Sussex in 2003. *(Empics)*

favourite with the Kent faithful, completed a 94-ball century that included thirteen fours and two sixes. Paul Nixon did not last long and at tea Kent were on 322 for 5. Symonds was out shortly after tea but Ealham and Golding added valuable runs in the final session. With Salisbury claiming Ealham and Min Patel to finish with 4 for 59, and Saqlain removing Amjad Khan and Martin Saggers in the space of 4 balls to complete a return of 5 for 122, Kent suddenly subsided from 371 for 6 to 374 all out,

Rikki Clarke in fine form against
Nottinghamshire in 2005. *(Empics)*

restoring a degree of balance to the contest. However, Kent must have felt very pleased with their day's work, particularly as they captured the wicket of Ian Ward just before the close.

The second day started disastrously for Surrey when, in humid and overcast conditions, they lost 3 quick wickets. Mark Butcher, joined by Ali Brown, mounted a counterattack but Butcher was dismissed with the score at 59. Adam Hollioake then launched an assault on the bowling although batting with a chipped index finger. Needing to score 224 to avoid being asked to follow on, Batty tried to stay with Hollioake but departed at 126. Saqlain came in and watched Hollioake at the other end carry on the fight but lost his wicket with 56 runs still needed. Ormond went at 184 and, as Ed Giddins came to the wicket, the follow-on looked almost a certainty. Knowing that he would be unlikely to receive anything more than passive support from his number eleven, Hollioake simply stepped up the ferocity of his attack, taking 22 runs from a Saggers over to complete a 95-ball century, his first in the Championship since September 1999, and then a couple more boundaries from Khan in the next over put his side within 2 runs of saving the follow-on. Khan then attempted to keep Hollioake off strike by delivering a bouncer, but the ball passed so high over the batsman's head that umpire Trevor Jesty was forced to call it a no ball, thereby enabling Surrey to achieve their objective. Giddins was dismissed in the next over, leaving Hollioake undefeated on 122 not out from 103 balls in a memorable innings.

Surrey still trailed by 149 runs as they took the field, minus their injured captain, to try to find their way back into the game. Giddins removed Fulton and Ormond dismissed Smith with just 33 runs on the board, but Key and Symonds quickly re-established Kent's superiority with a partnership of 97 that was only broken on the stroke of tea when Symonds was caught at short leg after completing a fine 52-ball

SURREY v. KENT

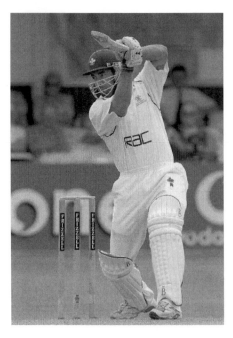

Adam Hollioake batting against Warwickshire in 2003.
(Empics)

half-century. Having gone to tea at a comfortable 135 for 3, Kent found themselves rather less well placed at 145 for 6 some 6 overs after the restart as Salisbury and Saqlain struck three times to leave them grateful for the contribution of Key, who completed a valuable fifty from 96 balls during this mini-collapse.

The extraordinary third day saw Kent bat through almost until lunch to reach a total of 260 and a lead of 409. The afternoon session started with Butcher being dropped, but he only lasted until the score passed 50 and 2 quick wickets fell at 54. Ian Ward was batting nicely and was well supported by Rikki Clarke, one of the newer players in the Surrey side. After tea he fell to a catch by Hockley and then Brown was given out on a dubious decision. All now rested on Hollioake, but he was caught at the wicket just before play stopped because of rain. This break lasted only nine minutes and Jonathan Batty was out just after the resumption. Ian Ward continued on to his century, ably supported by Saqlain, but Kent claimed the extra half-hour, hoping to complete the game on the third day, without success.

At the start of the fourth day Surrey were 264 for 7 and all expectations were of a Kent win. Ward and Saqlain had other ideas, although Saqlain survived an early chance to mid-on. Having played the major role in helping Ward to add 105 for the eighth wicket, which brought Surrey's target down below 100, he was mortified to give a straightforward catch to wide mid-on. All now depended on Jimmy Ormond to support Ian Ward and between them they saw off the new ball. Ward went on to register his highest personal score of 168 not out from an eight-hour marathon innings. By the mid-afternoon Surrey had clinched one of the greatest wins in the club's history, which sparked off celebrations on the visiting team's dressing room balcony and among the small group of away supporters who had optimistically stayed on in Canterbury.

Surrey's historic victory extended their lead at the top of the Championship table and proved to very significant in the race for the title. They went on to win the title by a clear 44.75 points from Warwickshire in second place and Kent in third.

SURREY v. KENT

Played at Canterbury on 19th, 20th, 21st and 22nd July 2002 [4-day Match]   Toss: Kent
Surrey won by 2 wickets

KENT

*D.P. Fulton	c Clarke b Saqlain	62	c Batty b Giddins	11
R.W.T. Key	lbw b Saqlain	57	c Batty b Ormond	68
E.T. Smith	run out (Clarke)	19	c Ramprakash b Ormond	6
A. Symonds	b Saqlain	118	c Ward b Saqlain	51
J.B. Hockley	st Batty b Salisbury	46	c Ward b Saqlain	8
#P.A. Nixon	c Giddins b Salisbury	8	c Batty b Saqlain	1
M.A. Ealham	c Batty b Salisbury	18	b Salisbury	0
J.M. Golding	not out	24	lbw b Giddins	26
M.M. Patel	b Salisbury	1	not out	43
A. Khan	lbw b Saqlain	1	lbw b Salisbury	11
M.J. Saggers	b Saqlain	0	lbw b Saqlain	2
Extras	b 6, lb 4, w 6, nb 4	20	b 5, lb 16, w 2, nb 15	33
Total	**(all out)**	**374**	**(all out)**	**260**

SURREY

M.A. Butcher	c Fulton b Khan	34	c Symonds b Saggers	7
I.J. Ward	c Nixon b Khan	7	not out	168
I.D.K. Salisbury	b Saggers	2	(8) b Ealham	5
M.R. Ramprakash	c Nixon b Saggers	0	(3) c Nixon b Saggers	2
R. Clarke	c Nixon b Khan	5	(4) c Hockley b Symonds	66
A.D. Brown	b Saggers	9	(5) c Ealham b Symonds	0
*A.J. Hollioake	not out	122	(6) c Nixon b Saggers	8
#J.N. Batty	c Symonds b Golding	8	(7) c Key b Symonds	0
Saqlain Mushtaq	b Saggers	4	c Patel b Khan	60
J. Ormond	b Khan	4	not out	43
E.S.H. Giddins	c Symonds b Saggers	1		
Extras	lb 13, w 2, nb 14	29	b 17, lb 13, w 2, nb 6	38
Total	**(all out)**	**225**	**(for 8 wickets)**	**410**

Bowling

SURREY	O	M	R	W	O	M	R	W
Giddins	17	5	39	0	15	3	40	2
Ormond	14	2	80	0	17	3	61	2
Clarke	8	0	56	0	4	0	23	0
Saqlain Mushtaq	33.5	8	122	5	19.5	3	60	4
Hollioake	2	0	8	0				
Salisbury	17	3	59	4	18	1	55	2

KENT	O	M	R	W	O	M	R	W
Saggers	13.5	3	66	5	31	6	85	3
Khan	16	2	91	4	20	3	91	1
Patel	6	3	21	0	20	6	50	0
Golding	8	2	13	1	8	1	27	0
Ealham	6	2	21	0	19.3	7	42	1
Symonds	1	1	0	0	28	5	85	3

FALL OF WICKETS

	K	S	K	S
1st	121	16	18	52
2nd	122	29	33	54
3rd	155	29	130	177
4th	285	34	142	181
5th	321	59	144	190
6th	329	77	145	191
7th	371	126	189	208
8th	373	169	203	313
9th	374	184	255	–
10th	374	225	260	–

Umpires: D.J. Constant and T.E. Jesty

Surrey v. Kent

Date: 25-28 May 2004   County Championship

Location: The Brit Oval

When Jon Batty clipped his twentieth four through mid-wicket to reach his hundred just after tea on the first day, Mark Ramprakash embraced him. Batty had been the flashing blade to Ramprakash's restrained play, captain and vice-captain, in an unbroken stand of 214 in 54 overs that put Surrey in control and could have had deep significance for the rest of the season.

Surrey had won for the first time in the season against Essex the previous Sunday in the Totesport League, but at 1 for 2 after 4 overs, with Mohammad Sami and Martin Saggers champing at the bit, it did not look as if they had turned a corner. Kent, the Championship leaders, smelt blood. Batty dropped himself down the order and Nadeem Shahid came into the team as opener. He did not last long, edging Sami to one of two gullies in the third over. Scott Newman was unlucky to be judged leg-before in the next over to one from Saggers that swung back into the left-hander. As Ramprakash was averaging a hundred every five first-class games it was no surprise that he should score his first of the season in his sixth championship game. It came off 185 balls.

Rikki Clarke provided a temporary partner. Dropped on 20 by Amjad Khan off his own bowling, he was out just before lunch edging to second slip. Batty faced one torrid spell against Sami in the afternoon, but once through that he took the other bowlers apart. Particularly strong square of the wicket, it should have been his undoing on 87 when he uppercut Sami straight to Michael Carberry at backward point,

Mark Ramprakash batting against Warwickshire at Whitgift School during his purple patch for Surrey. *(Empics)*

but the chance was spilt. Batty completed his seventh first-class hundred after tea off 145 balls, the last 69 off 61 balls. But after initially refusing the bad light he was quick to leave the field when the ball was thrown to Sami in the gloom.

On the second day, resuming on 306 for 3, Surrey would have been disappointed only to get to 479. Kent bowled well in the morning to remove both the century makers and then, after lunch, Surrey self-destructed looking for quick runs. Batty added just 9 to his overnight score before he was out trying an ambitious scoop against Khan and hit it straight to mid-wicket. It was Sami's speed with the new ball that accounted for a well-set Ramprakash. He was nearly flattened by a bouncer from the Pakistan bowler coming round the wicket before, next ball, being rushed into a pull that he dragged on to his stumps. Alistair Brown and Azhar Mahmood steadied things and Brown went to his second fifty of the season, but wickets fell to the hitherto harmless slow left-arm bowling of Rob Ferley.

However, Surrey seized the initiative with 2 wickets in the final 2 overs to leave Kent on the ropes still needing 149 runs to avoid the follow-on. It was another fantastic

Jonathan Batty claiming his eighth catch for a new record off the bowling of Martin Bicknell in this match. *(Empics)*

day for Jonathan Batty, who followed his hundred by taking all 5 wickets caught behind. Without Robert Key, Kent would have been in real trouble. While others had their techniques worked over by Azhar Mahmood, moving the ball both ways in the air and off the pitch from the Pavilion End, Key stood resolute, leaving well and hitting immaculately straight. Key took 140 balls to reach 50 but Kent will thank him for the sweat. When Michael Carberry was caught down the leg side in the penultimate over of the day, Surrey seized the initiative and rammed it home when Martin Saggers, the nightwatchman, was also caught down the leg side by Batty off Rikki Clarke.

On the third day Batty moved easily to his right to catch Mohammad Sami, the last man, off Martin Bicknell to ensure Kent followed on. In doing so, he bettered Arnold Long's Surrey record of seven catches against Sussex at Hove in 1964. In fact he had caught eight and by scoring a century became only the second wicketkeeper in first-class history to achieve this feat, the other being Steve Marsh of Kent at Lord's in 1991.

Kent lasted only 15 overs and added only 58 to their overnight 181 for 5. Key inside-edged a drive off Bicknell and the rest followed meekly to Rikki Clarke and Bicknell. Kent followed on 240 behind and were soon in trouble when David Fulton middled one straight to mid-wicket. Ed Smith played on and Matthew Walker was leg-before offering no stroke. Key's cover-driving on the up against Jimmy Ormond was a joy to watch. His fifty came at a run-per-ball and then he dropped anchor, taking another 105 to reach his fifth first-class hundred of the season in his tenth innings. Key and Carberry, who was dropped badly at second slip on 9 by Azhar Mahmood, put on 126 in 56 overs, but Carberry edged Ormond in his second over of off breaks to slip twenty-five minutes before the close.

SURREY v. KENT

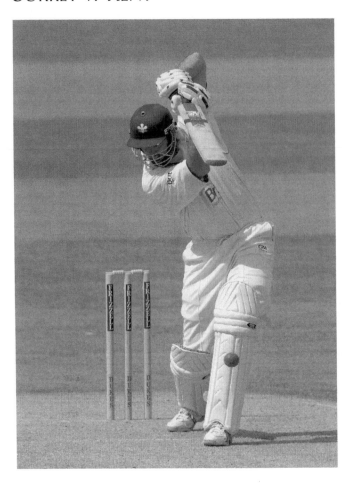

Martin Bicknell showing his skill with the bat against Nottinghamshire at The Brit Oval in 2005. *(Empics)*

On the last day the Kent tail wagged briefly but Surrey, needing 174 off a minimum of 47 overs, knocked them off with 12.3 overs to spare. Kent lost only 1 wicket before lunch and, with Key at the crease and being 114 ahead, looked like saving the game. During an over smashing Rikki Clarke around, Key went past his previous best but he was tiring and after driving Bicknell uppishly for two consecutive fours he lunged at an away-swinger and edged to first slip to be out on 199. He had fielded for nine hours and been at the crease for twelve hours and seven minutes over his two innings. Amjad Khan and Mohammad Sami added 49 in 41 balls for the last wicket, but that only served to suggest how easy Surrey's chase would be. Martin Bicknell took the forty-first five-wicket haul of his career, including his 1,000th first-class wicket, in his nineteenth season for Surrey. It came in the fourth over of the morning when Matthew Dennington pushed forward and nicked one behind. It was fitting, though, that Jonathan Batty hit the winning boundary and that Mark Ramprakash added an unbeaten 91 to his 157 in the first innings.

Surrey had experienced a diabolical start to the season but their strength in depth got them out of trouble, and 4 wins out of their last 5 matches saw them finish in a clear third place.

SURREY v. KENT

Played at The Brit Oval on 25th, 26th, 27th and 28th May 2004 [4-day Match]   Toss: Surrey
Surrey won by 7 wickets

SURREY

S.A. Newman	lbw b Saggers	0	c Saggers b Carberry		31
N. Shahid	c Smith b Mohammad Sami	1	lbw b Saggers		0
M.R. Ramprakash	b Mohammad Sami	157	not out		91
R. Clarke	c Walker b Saggers	44	c Saggers b Walker		15
*#J.N. Batty	c Ferley b Khan	129	not out		18
A.D. Brown	st O'Brien b Ferley	79			
A.J. Hollioake	lbw b Amjad Khan	2			
Azhar Mahmood	b Ferley	27			
M.P. Bicknell	c Smith b Ferley	6			
J. Ormond	c O'Brien b Saggers	6			
Zaheer Khan	not out	2			
Extras	b 10, lb 3, w 1, nb 12	26	b 6, lb 3, nb 10		19
Total	**(all out)**	**479**	**(for 3 wickets)**		**174**

KENT

*D.P. Fulton	c Batty b Azhar Mahmood	30	c sub b Azhar Mahmood		13
R.W.T. Key	c Batty b Bicknell	86	c Brown b Bicknell		199
E.T. Smith	c Batty b Azhar Mahmood	25	b Ormond		23
M.J. Walker	c Batty b Azhar Mahmood	20	lbw b Bicknell		0
M.A. Carberry	c Batty b Azhar Mahmood	17	c Brown b Ormond		61
M.J. Saggers	c Batty b Clarke	1	(10) b Bicknell		0
M.J. Dennington	b Clarke	11	(6) c Batty b Bicknell		12
#N.J. O'Brien	c Brown b Clarke	15	(7) c Batty b Clarke		21
R.S. Ferley	c Batty b Bicknell	0	(8) lbw b Bicknell		4
Amjad Khan	not out	9	(9) not out		22
Mohammad Sami	c Batty b Bicknell	5	c Shahid b Khan		29
Extras	b 1, lb 6, w 1, nb 12	20	b 1, lb 14, nb 14		29
Total	**(all out)**	**239**	**(all out)**		**413**

Bowling

KENT	O	M	R	W	O	M	R	W
Mohammad Sami	24	6	75	2	3	0	24	0
Saggers	31.1	6	111	3	4	1	9	1
Dennington	21	5	71	0	6	0	21	0
Amjad Khan	27	3	102	0	2.3	0	20	0
Ferley	24	2	107	3				
Carberry					12	0	67	1
Walker					7	0	24	1

SURREY	O	M	R	W	O	M	R	W
Khan	11	2	53	0	15.4	0	48	1
Bicknell	21.4	6	51	3	34	8	128	5
Ormond	15	5	25	0	44	14	97	2
Azhar Mahmood	15	5	56	4	22	5	63	1
Clarke	11	2	47	3	14	2	49	1
Ramprakash					2	0	7	0
Brown					2	1	6	0

FALL OF WICKETS

	S	K	K	S
1st	1	52	26	14
2nd	1	82	109	81
3rd	92	142	114	116
4th	323	180	240	–
5th	379	181	272	–
6th	386	199	313	–
7th	440	203	361	–
8th	464	204	364	–
9th	477	220	364	–
10th	479	239	413	–

Umpires: I.J. Gould and B. Leadbeater

SURREY v. GLAMORGAN

Date: 11-14 May 2005   County Championship
Location: The Brit Oval

With the advent of overseas players and Kolpak cricketers arriving in county cricket it was pleasing to note that in this match twenty-one of those involved were qualified to play for England, eleven of them from Wales, and the twenty-second, Mohammad Akram, was qualified for county cricket by residence.

After Surrey won the toss and elected to bat Glamorgan took 2 wickets with the new ball, but by the time they left the field, Brown had hit a typically blistering hundred in the wake of a relatively sedate one by Scott Newman and a commanding 84 by Rikki Clarke. Brown's thirty-seventh first-class hundred took him 95 balls. Leg-before working to leg, he had hit two of the day's sixes and twenty-one of the sixty-five fours.

Glamorgan started well on the second day by hurrying through Surrey's last 3 wickets, but Martin Bicknell took only 5 balls to find that ideal length that made him so dangerous whenever he had a new ball in his hands. Constantly hitting the seam, as usual, from his model action, he went on to take 6 wickets, the forty-second time he had taken 5 wickets in an innings in his career. In the second innings he went on to take his 1,000th wicket for the county, the fifteenth Surrey player to achieve this feat.

Batting that lacked application and judgement made it seem that Glamorgan would face the possibility of being asked to follow-on, but Harrison kept his side in the game with some hearty pulling and driving in his innings of 75 not out, completed in 73 balls, which left the deficit on first innings at 99 runs.

On day three Scott Newman became the first batsman in Surrey's history to register a century and double-century in the same match. His 219, coupled with his 117 in the first innings, was devalued only to an extent by the Harleyford Road boundary, fifty-eight yards from the pitch to its closest point. Four-day cricket has an unfair advantage but only Bobby Abel and W.W. Read have made more runs in a game for the county, both in a single innings at the end of the nineteenth century. Newman hit the ball hard and handsomely, using his height to drive with the straightest of bats, and never missed the chance to play the pull shot. He gave not a chance until top-edging a pull to mid-on, having hit twenty-eight fours and four sixes.

Scott Newman batting to enter the record books. *(Empics)*

Mark Ramprakash batted without semblance of error on his way to what seemed sure to be his fourth hundred in as many championship matches, but he was bowled by the spirited Andrew Davies, working to leg, 4 overs before Newman left to a standing ovation and the congratulations of admirably courteous opponents. It brought no respite as Alistair Brown and Rikki Clarke continued to plunder runs, with Brown in 22 balls hitting five fours and two sixes. Surrey declared, setting Glamorgan a target of 525 but they lost 2 quick wickets before the close on a day that saw a total of 536 runs scored.

On the last day Hemp and Powell continued to score freely but, after adding 171 for the third wicket, Powell fell to Ormond just 7 short of his century, and then Hemp became the first of Akram's 4 victims a mere 5 runs short of a hundred. With the help of Rikki Clarke, the last 7 wickets fell for 28 runs in 33 balls to see Surrey home to a comfortable victory. This helped to raise hopes for the season but Surrey managed only 2 more victories in the year and were relegated to Division Two by the slimmest margin of 1 point.

SURREY *v.* GLAMORGAN

Played at The Brit Oval on 11th, 12th, 13th and 14th May 2005 [4-day Match]   Toss: Surrey
Surrey won by 276 runs

SURREY

S.A. Newman	b Croft	117	c Croft b Davies		219
R.S. Clinton	c Wallace b Harrison	1	b Croft		24
*M.R. Ramprakash	b Harrison	2	b Davies		97
R. Clarke	c Wallace b Davies	84	lbw b S.D. Thomas		34
#J.N. Batty	c & b Cosker	25			
A.D. Brown	lbw b Cosker	122	[5] not out		42
J.G.E. Benning	c Hughes b Harrison	57			
M.P. Bicknell	not out	17			
J. Ormond	c I.J. Thomas b Davies	2			
N.D. Doshi	b Davies	0			
M. Akram	lbw b Croft	0			
Extras	lb 7, w 4, nb 6	17	lb 8, w 1		9
Total	**(all out)**	**444**	**(for 4 wickets declared)**		**425**

GLAMORGAN

I.J. Thomas	lbw b Bicknell	4	[2] c Newman b Bicknell		12
D.D. Cherry	lbw b Bicknell	47	[1] c Clarke b Bicknell		0
D.L. Hemp	lbw b Bicknell	24	c Batty b Akram		95
M.J. Powell	b Ormond	43	c Bicknell b Ormond		93
J. Hughes	b Clarke	30	b Clarke		6
#M.A. Wallace	c Batty b Bicknell	5	c sub (Salisbury) b Akram		0
*R.D.B. Croft	c Batty b Akram	27	c Brown b Akram		7
S.D. Thomas	c Batty b Clarke	12	c Batty b Clarke		2
D.S. Harrison	not out	75	b Clarke		0
D.A. Cosker	c Batty b Bicknell	17	b Akram		12
A.P. Davies	b Bicknell	37	not out		0
Extras	b 1, lb 5, nb 18	24	lb 10, w 1, nb 10		21
Total	**(all out)**	**345**	**(all out)**		**248**

Bowling

GLAMORGAN	O	M	R	W	O	M	R	W
Harrison	20	6	72	3	14	4	45	0
Davies	24	4	121	3	15	1	76	2
Croft	29.4	3	116	2	29	5	125	1
S.D. Thomas	0.3	0	8	0	13.3	1	84	1
Cosker	34.3	3	120	2	20	1	87	0

SURREY	O	M	R	W	O	M	R	W
Bicknell	19.5	3	74	6	17	5	55	2
Ormond	18	7	45	1	12	3	47	1
Clarke	9	0	61	2	8	1	46	3
Akram	17	3	98	1	12.1	1	63	4
Doshi	9	2	32	0	6	0	27	0
Benning	2	0	29	0				

FALL OF WICKETS

	S	G	S	G
1st	9	4	76	4
2nd	25	32	330	19
3rd	210	125	359	190
4th	210	143	425	220
5th	295	165	–	224
6th	409	169	–	224
7th	433	191	–	227
8th	443	233	–	227
9th	443	301	–	233
10th	444	345	–	248

Umpires: M.J. Harris and T.E. Jesty

Other cricket titles published by Tempus

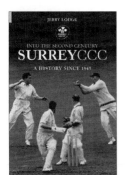

Into The Second Century Surrey CCC: A History Since 1945
JERRY LODGE

Celebrating their centenary just seven days after the Second World War, the county club has won more County Championships than anyone else since 1945. This delightful book contains comprehensive statistical information and over 100 superb illustrations.
0 7524 3177 3

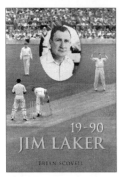

Jim Laker 19-90
BRIAN SCOVELL

This is the untold story of one of England's greatest cricketers, the Yorkshire-born off-spinner Jim Laker, written on the fiftieth anniversary of his greatest achievement, his 19-90 against the Australians at Old Trafford, a record that will probably never be beaten. Brian Scovell presents a fascinating new insight into the life of a courageous and misunderstood man.
0 7524 3932 4

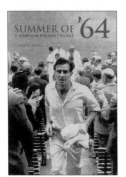

Summer of '64 A Season in English Cricket
ANDREW HIGNELL

The summer of 1964 saw Tom Graveney and Geoffrey Boycott make over 2,000 runs, while Derek Shackleton, Tom Cartwright, Fred Titmus and Ray Illingworth all produced outstanding bowling performances. Australia were the tourists and they narrowly won the Ashes series. The County Championship was keenly contested and Worcestershire managed to win the title. This nostalgic look at one of the finest seasons on record is packed with superb illustrations and is a book that any cricket fan will enjoy.

0 7524 3404 7

Wealding the Willow
ROBIN WHITCOMB

The Weald area of South-East England has long been known as the 'cradle of cricket'. Robin Whitcomb has travelled round the counties of Kent, Surrey, Hampshire and East and West Sussex visiting communities, collecting anecdotes and photographing the cricket. With a foreword by the much-loved Australian Test cricketer and commentator Richie Benaud, this is a worthy record of the great game and the places where it all began.

0 7524 3457 8

If you are interested in purchasing other books published by Tempus, or in case you have difficulty finding any Tempus books in your local bookshop, you can also place orders directly through our website

www.tempus-publishing.com